The Poverty **of Welfare Reform**

The Poverty of Welfare Reform

Joel F. Handler

Yale University Press New Haven and London

Designed by Rebecca Gibb.
Set in Minion type by The Composing Room of Michigan, Inc., Grand Rapids, Michigan.
Printed in the United States of America by BookCrafters, Inc., Chelsea, Michigan.

Library of Congress Cataloging-in-Publication Data

Handler, Joel F.
The poverty of welfare reform / Joel F. Handler.
p. cm.
Includes bibliographical references and index.
ISBN 0-300-06480-2 (alk. paper). — ISBN 0-300-06481-0 (pbk. : alk. paper)
1. Public welfare—United States. 2. Poverty—United States.
I. Title.
HV95.H2595 1995
362.5′0973—dc20 95-18630
CIP

A catalogue record for this book is available from the British Library.

The paper in this book meets the guidelines for permanence and durability of the Committee on Production Guidelines for Book Longevity of the Council on Library Resources.

10 9 8 7 6 5 4 3 2

For Betsy, and Mark and Anne, Alan and Rose Marie

Contents

Acknowledgments

I wish to thank Mark Greenberg, Yeheskel Hasenfeld, and Lucy Williams for their continuing support and great help. Katherine Hill provided valuable research assistance. Margaret Kiever is a great secretary and a good friend. This book is part of a larger project, written with Yeheskel Hasenfeld, tentatively entitled *The Organization of Welfare: Dilemmas and Solutions,* generously supported by the Twentieth Century Fund.

The Poverty of Welfare Reform

1 Welfare and Poverty

Once again, America is getting tough on welfare. Although there are many assistance programs for the poor, when people say "welfare," they mean Aid to Families with Dependent Children (AFDC)—the program essentially for single mothers and their children. As a presidential candidate Bill Clinton promised to "end welfare as we know it," and as president he introduced the Work and Responsibility Act of 1994. In that same session of Congress, Republicans introduced an even tougher measure. Meanwhile, during the Reagan, Bush, and Clinton administrations, the states, acting under federal waivers, have significantly reformed welfare. The battle over welfare reform escalated in 1995 with the new Republican-controlled Congress. Republicans again right-flanked Democrats with even tougher welfare provisions than Democrats proposed. The states, too, have increased their demands to deal with welfare free from federal interference. In short, getting tough on welfare continues to be good politics at both the state and the national level. Given the considerable overlap between the Democratic and Republican legislative proposals, as well as state reforms, there appears to be a broad consensus on what is wrong with welfare. Aside from "getting tough," however, there is little agreement on what to do about welfare and the division of responsibilities between the states and the federal government. It seems safe to conclude that the country will continue to reform welfare over the next several years.

Four factors—whether real or perceived—have historically produced crises over welfare: increases in public costs and threats to the work ethic, family values, and social order. Although the shape and intensity of these factors have varied at different times, they seem to be always present in one form or another and are clearly present today. Welfare rolls and costs have been increasing. In a few states, tough reforms are being pushed even though costs are not in fact rising, because taxpayers still resent paying public funds to recipients. Because of perceived threats to the work ethic, family values, and the social order, the cost, whatever it is, is too great.

The distinguishing characteristic of the three other factors is that they threaten fundamental values: they are moral issues. Welfare, many now believe, is no longer a temporary measure to help single mothers and their children over a bad patch. Instead, it encourages and perpetuates dependency. It has become "a way of life" and therefore compromises the work ethic. Both the Democratic and Republican legislative proposals, as well as several of the states' agendas, place time limits on welfare. A consensus is forming that welfare should last no longer than two years. Disputes are whether the recipient will receive education and training during that time or be immediately pushed into work and whether, at the end of two years, the recipient will be completely cut off or required to take a job in either the private or the public sector as a condition of receiving aid. In any event, welfare, it is agreed, will be changed dramatically.

Proposals to place time limits on welfare may sound like they come from the right. Actually, they come from the liberal left. True, during the Reagan years, prominent conservatives attacked the idea of entitlement and argued that citizens had *responsibilities.* The "truly needy" deserve to be helped, they argued, but they must also contribute to society by supporting themselves and their families if they can. This is the social contract.[1] The theme of responsibility became very popular and is now also endorsed by liberals. Dependent mothers will be helped—by income and by education and training—but after a reasonable period of time, they must help themselves.[2]

Liberals used to state that the welfare mother's responsibility was to stay at home and take care of her children, but times have changed. Today's argument is that because the majority of women, including mothers of young children, are now in the paid labor force, welfare mothers can no longer expect to stay home and take care of their children. Just as mothers not on welfare are now expected to work in the paid labor force, so, too, are welfare mothers expected to work.

Throughout history, failures of the able-bodied to support themselves and their families have not only compromised the work ethic but have spilled over into other areas of personal and family life. The "unworthy" poor have always been associated with sin, vice, disease, and crime. Adults who can work but do not are deviant. They fail as role models, jeopardizing the appropriate socialization of their children. In addition, today's welfare mothers do not marry but have children out-of-wedlock and engage in other forms of antisocial behavior, including drugs and crime. The result is that welfare children grow up in poverty; they suffer from bad environments, do poorly in school, and often follow the paths of their parents in dependency or worse.

Race, ethnicity, and religion reinforce the moral condemnation. In a prior age, the unworthy poor were the "dangerous classes."[3] Now the euphemism is "counterculture poverty." The stereotypical welfare recipient is a young, inner-city black mother who has several children in order to get more welfare, thus breeding another generation of future welfare mothers, unemployed males, and criminals. In prior periods of welfare crises, threats to the social order often involved riots or the fear of riots; today, Americans fear the "underclass."[4]

Self-sufficiency through work strengthens important family values. But the cluster of proposed and recently enacted family values reforms deal with other issues of social behavior—refusing to support children conceived while their mothers were on welfare, banning aid to children born to unmarried teens, requiring teen mothers to live with their parents, encouraging marriage, restricting migration, and requiring birth control, immunizations, and attendance at school.

Behind the consensus on the welfare crisis lie several key assumptions about the nature of poverty and its cures:

- "Dependency," as used in the context of welfare, is not simply being poor. It is not simply being out of work. Rather, welfare dependency is a moral issue; it is a failure to have the proper work ethic.
- Providing aid destroys the work ethic. Welfare is not simply a matter of "economics"—that is, providing income support. Rather, fundamental values are threatened.
- The behavior of the individual rather than the environment should be changed. Self-sufficiency through work is to be achieved by changing the mothers rather than the labor market. People who want to work can work.
- Reform efforts should be directed at adults. In spite of the apparent fear that deviant values will be passed on, with relatively few exceptions (for example, requiring school attendance), welfare children are largely ignored.

The current welfare reforms, both enacted and proposed, are being hailed as "new"; their proponents claim that now welfare will really be changed. This sort of political rhetoric, of course, accompanies most legislative change. In fact, both the underlying assumptions about poverty and welfare reform seem to be timeless. In chapter 2, I provide a brief historical overview of welfare, showing the incredible continuity of the basic assumptions about what is wrong with public assistance for the poor and what can be done about it. In an interesting coincidence, the new round of welfare reforms, if passed, will take hold just a couple of years shy of the 650th anniversary of the Statute of Laborers (1349). That statute, enacted in England during the reign of Edward III, is usually considered the first legislation on welfare—the start of "social security."[5] The ongoing similarities between welfare reform at the close of the twentieth century and the previous half a millennium are striking. Both the "menace" of welfare and its "cures" have not really changed. Welfare policy, as we shall see, still lies in the shadow of the sturdy beggar. Either the historical analysis and approach must be very good ideas to have lasted this long, or, as I shall argue, it's time we rethought these issues.

In chapter 2, I analyze aid to single mothers and their children—AFDC—during the development of the American welfare state. Contrary to popular impressions, poor, single mothers and their children, with rare exceptions, were considered part of the "unworthy" or "undeserving" poor in that they were never excused from the paid labor market. At the same time, they were condemned for working because they violated patriarchal norms. Throughout the history of welfare, people of color or those of different religions or national origins suffered the additional burden of discrimination. The harsh characteristics of AFDC, as well as its predecessor, Aid to Dependent Children (ADC), reflected the unworthy status of single mothers and their children, as compared to programs that aided the "deserving" poor. Welfare for single mothers and their children has always been accompanied by work requirements.

Today, most nonwelfare mothers are in the paid labor force. But now the tables are reversed, and welfare mothers are condemned for not being able to support themselves and their families through paid labor. The remedy, the ultimate work enforcement mechanism, is to cut off welfare to force these dependents back into the paid labor force. This is the oldest remedy of all. Today we call it time-limited welfare.

I next turn to the contemporary approach to welfare reform. Paid labor, the argument goes, is preferable to welfare for a number of important reasons—material well-being, autonomy, the socialization of children. People define themselves in terms of their work. Yet there are a lot of things wrong with the current approach to welfare reform. My argument is different. "Ending welfare as we know it" draws the distinction between "welfare" and "work," and this idea is no longer credible. To frame welfare reform policy in terms of moving recipients from welfare to the paid labor force is to fail to define the problem; it perpetuates past myths and mistakes, including again, blaming the victims: poor, single mothers and their children.

In chapters 3 and 4, I make three points: (1) although welfare has lots of problems, the essential problem is poverty, which is much broader and more serious than welfare; (2) for the past twenty years, and in the current debate, "work" is still conceived of as a full-time steady career employment at decent wages and with benefits; this is becoming increasingly untrue for significant portions of the labor force, who are less-than-full-time employees; and (3) large numbers of welfare recipients—perhaps the majority—are already in the labor force; trying to move them to "work," when it is more than likely minimum-wage, less-than-full-time employment, will neither solve the poverty problem nor significantly reduce welfare. Better directions exist as part of the Clinton administration's program, but they are not welfare reform.

A great many state welfare-to-work demonstration projects have been conducted over the past several years. These projects have been evaluated primarily by the Manpower Development Research Corporation (MDRC), a respected and skilled organization, and the reports have received much publicity. The MDRC has approved some of the more important projects—"work programs can work"—and MDRC reports have become influential in welfare reform policy debates. I analyze some of the more important projects and reports in chapter 4 and argue that the success rates of even the "successful" projects have been exaggerated; most participants do not even approach self-sufficiency. The MDRC reports point out the important qualifications that are lost in the political debates. As a result, key elements of some of the state demonstration projects now represent the future of welfare-to-work reform.

In chapter 5, I look at states' efforts to reform welfare so as to strengthen "family values." The allocation of authority among units of government has always played a major role in social welfare programs. That allocation corresponds to the moral characteristics of the class of poor being helped. Programs for the deserving poor—those who are morally excused from work—tend to be administered at the national level. Those for deviants, the undeserving poor, are handled at the state and local levels. This distribution of welfare programs results primarily from two causes: first, moral conflicts are felt most keenly in local communities, and those communities want to keep control over deviant behavior; second, upper levels of government delegate authority to lower levels to avoid conflict. Thus, there tends to be agreement that conflicts over welfare are best handled at the local level. Aid to Dependent Children and its successor, AFDC, were handled for decades at primarily the state and local levels. During the 1960s and 1970s, federal AFDC requirements were enacted in certain limited areas, particularly eligibility and work requirements, but, as I argue, the federal influence was in fact never very great. As welfare has now become a crisis over moral values, we are witnessing a return to state power. Today there is no such thing as a national AFDC program; in fact, if one considers the tremendous discretion available to local offices, there are not even fifty state AFDC programs. It is in this highly decentralized context that one must consider all current reform proposals, especially those from Washington.

Current reform proposals, whether Democratic, Republican, or state-sponsored—the subject of chapter 6—not only misconceive the power of Washington to control welfare administration, but also seriously misconceive the nature of the welfare population—who the recipients are, why they are on welfare, how long they are on welfare, and how they get off welfare—as well as what to do to for welfare mothers and their children. In light of the characteristics of the population and what they need, it is hard to think of more inappropriate legislation. The disjuncture between what is legislated and what is needed, is, of course, not new. As we shall see, social policy has been stuck on the same misconceptions for almost 650 years.

What is the likely outcome of present efforts to reform welfare? I address this question in chapter 7. In the past, at least the recent past, legislated reforms are usually ignored, and life goes on for the poor without much change—there is neither much improvement because of the legislation nor much sanctioning for failure to comply. There are two basic reasons for this outcome. First, it is usually more costly in the short run to institute work or other reform programs than simply to keep families on welfare, and state and local governments think in the short run. Second, if welfare officials get too tough on mothers, state and local governments will have to pick up the pieces—more impoverishment, more need for health care, more broken homes, and more children in foster care, which is more expensive than welfare. To be sure, welfare is always changing, but that is caused by changes in local economies. I still think that this will happen with the current reforms, but I am less confident. Several new provisions in the proposed federal legislation not only purport to close loopholes but also change fiscal incentives at the state level. It may soon be to the financial advantage of state and local governments to impose sanctions on welfare families.

What is going on? Why does society cling to the basic assumptions that underlie welfare policy when it is so clear that they do not comport with reality? Why do we perpetuate the same misguided policies that not only do nothing positive for the welfare poor but continue to punish and stigmatize them? What is this incessant need to blame the victim? Why do we continue this exercise in symbolic politics? Welfare policy, I argue, is not addressed to the poor—it is addressed to us. It is an affirmation of majoritarian values through the creation of deviants. The poor are held hostage to make sure that the rest of us behave. This is clearly illustrated in the history of welfare policy, to which we now turn.

"It is not bread the poor need, it is soul; it is not soup, it is spirit."

2 The Past Is Prologue

The Statute of Laborers, enacted in 1349 in England during the reign of Edward III, is usually considered the first legislation on welfare—the start of "social security."[1] The key section of the statute reads: "Because that many valiant beggars, as long as they may live of begging, do refuse to labor, giving themselves to idleness and vice, and sometimes to theft and other abominations; none upon said pain of imprisonment, shall under the color of pity or alms, give anything to such, which may labor, or presume to favor them towards their desires, so that thereby they may be compelled to labor for their necessary living." This statute, in other words, was an attempt to force beggars to seek work by preventing the giving of alms—in other words, by cutting off welfare.

What precipitated this action? By the middle of the fourteenth century, begging, a widespread and generally accepted behavior, had become a social problem. Feudalism was giving way to capitalism, the woolen industry had been introduced, land was being foreclosed, and employed labor was replacing serfdom. Working people were losing the security of the manor, and during periods of economic dislocation, they roamed the countryside and migrated to towns in search of work. The general climate was one of social upheaval. Migratory, transient workers, landholders claimed, led to growing mendacity and crime. Landlords were losing control over their labor, and they feared threats to their safety and property. The more immediate cause of the statute was an acute labor shortage, induced first by a famine and then by the Black Death (1348–49), which claimed a third of the population. As a result, wages began to rise. In addition to prohibiting the giving of alms, the statute sought to restrict laborers' movement, require them to work, and fix their wages. In other words—and this is the key point—the first statute to deal with "social security" was not about poverty and destitution. Rather, it was about the labor market.[2]

Capitalism, wage labor, and poverty continued to grow. Subsequent statutes filled out the basic contours of English welfare policy. It was recognized that certain categories of the poor were outside the labor market—the aged, the impotent, the sick, feeble, and lame. For this class, the work ethic, or moral behavior, was not at issue. At first, the "worthy poor" were given licenses to beg in designated locations; then publicly gathered alms were provided so that they would not have to beg. Children caught begging were apprenticed.

The able-bodied received very different treatment. Idleness was the "mother and root of all vices." Once again, in response to growing cries of beggary and vagabondage, those who "be lusty or having limbs strong enough to labor" were to be kept in "continual labor." By Elizabethan times, work was provided—as training, to prevent "roguery," as a test of "good intent," and to provide employment for the needy. Administration was local. Strangers were sent away. Those who violated statutory requirements were imprisoned.[3]

These basic English poor law principles—direct aid for the unemployable, work (or imprisonment) for the able-bodied, and local administration—influenced welfare policy in colonial North America.[4] Rapid and profound economic changes, periodic depressions, fluctuations in immigration and seasonal and wage labor, low wages (even lower for women), lack of public transportation, sickness and disease, old people without families—all contributed to serious poverty in the colonies. There were no clear lines between the destitute and the ordinary working family. There was no income support to cushion unexpected job loss or injury. The rapidly growing cities were becoming home to increasing numbers of beggars, tramps, criminals, and misfits.[5]

By the mid-seventeenth century, several colonies had enacted poor laws patterned after English legislation. There were four basic responses to poverty: auctioning off the poor ("selling" them to the lowest bidder, who agreed to care for and maintain them with public funds), contracting the poor (placing them in private homes at public expense), outdoor relief (basic assistance given outside the confines of a public institution), and the poorhouse (public institutions, also known as indoor relief). Administration was at the smallest unit of government.

Communities responded to the needs of friends and neighbors; they were decidedly less generous to strangers, and as transiency increased, attempts were made to restrict movement and immigration. Strangers were asked to post bond as a condition of settling; those who were thought likely to become dependent were "warned away"—told to leave. If they returned, they were severely punished.[6]

Although most colonists acknowledged the need to care for those unable to care for themselves, again, matters were quite different for the able-bodied. Religion (work was virtuous, idleness sinful), the need to hold down taxes, and the need for labor meant, in no uncertain terms, that those who could work should work. As Cotton Mather put it, "For those who indulge themselves in idleness, the express command of God unto us is, that we should let them starve."[7] As in

England, there was a clear difference between being poor and being a pauper. Pauperdom was a moral issue. The idle able-bodied were viewed as criminals, threats to themselves and the community. They were either bound out as indentured servants, whipped and expelled, or jailed. By the beginning of the eighteenth century, paupers were confined to workhouses, and their children were apprenticed. Putting the pauper to work was considered beneficial to both the pauper and the community.

After the Revolution, and throughout the nineteenth century, the major policy concern about welfare was outdoor relief. This form of aid came to be considered a principal cause of pauperism. Writing in 1835, and reflecting the received wisdom of the day, Alexis de Tocqueville, while admiring the generosity of the English in devoting resources to help the poor, severely criticized the English relief system in his "Memoir on Pauperism." Man had a "natural passion for idleness," which, for the majority, could be overcome only "by the need to live." This was the Malthusian view that humans were by nature slothful and could be impelled to work only by the "direst necessity." The relief system was destructive: by providing the means of subsistence, it relieved the poor of the obligation to work. Tocqueville condemned other evils of public outdoor relief: it debased the poor and destroyed the bonds of society, and in practice, it was impossible to separate the worthy from the unworthy. Tocqueville buttressed his arguments with examples of fraud and abuse now familiar to his readers.[8]

By the 1820s and 1830s, in both England and the United States, reformers began to advocate poorhouses as the principal form of poor relief. Poorhouses, or workhouses or almshouses, already existed in several American cities, but there was a new emphasis on making the poorhouse either the exclusive (in England) or the primary method of relief.

In the United States, the rise of the poorhouse was part of a broader institutional movement. Specialized institutions, reformers argued, would be created to deal with specific social problems—the mentally ill, juvenile delinquents, criminals. The theory was that crime, pauperism, ignorance, and mental illness were only different manifestations of an underlying "pathological condition of dependence" caused by "environmental factors," such as a dysfunctional family or the lack of religion or proper education. Institutional life would not only protect the individual from corrupting influences but also allow the individual to reform. Poorhouses were similarly conceived: "They would suppress intemperance, the primary cause of pauperism, and inculcate the habit of steady work."[9]

As always, fueling the drive for substituting the poorhouse for outdoor relief was the rise of pauperism, threats to the social order, rising public expenses, and concerns about the supply of labor. England's famous Royal Poor Law Commission Report of 1834 reiterated the basic moral distinction between poverty and pauperism. Whereas it acknowledged several causes of *poverty*—urbanization, immigration, and intemperance—it maintained that the primary cause of *pauperism* was the indiscriminate giving of aid, which destroyed the desire to work. "Paupers were living proof that a modestly comfortable life could be had without hard labor."[10] From this premise there followed the important doctrine of "less eligibility"—that is, "that the condition of welfare recipients, regardless of need or cause, should be worse than that of the lowest paid self-supporting laborer. While relief should not be denied the poor, life should be made so miserable for them that they would rather work than accept public aid."[11] As we shall see, welfare policy today continues to lie in the shadow of the doctrine of "less eligibility."

But why did the Elizabethan poor laws have to be reformed? Poor relief was only to be given to those who could not work; the able-bodied were required to work as a condition of receiving aid. The reason was administrative. It was too difficult in practice to distinguish the malingerer from the disabled—"the nuances which separate unmerited misfortune from an adversity produce by vice." As Gertrude Himmelfarb quotes, "Character and circumstance were too intimately related, misery and vice too much a part of each other, to lend themselves to such distinctions. Besides, even if they could be distinguished, what magistrate would let a poor man die because it was his own fault he was dying?"[12] There were other problems with the Elizabethan poor laws—issues that resonate today. When relief became a "right" and the poor could count on it as "income," all "stimulus to industry and economy" was "annihilated or weakened." "The just pride of independence, so honorable to a man, in every condition," was "corrupted by the certainty of public provision."[13]

The poorhouse (called workhouse in the poor law report) would maintain the principle of less eligibility while avoiding the pitfalls of attempting to draw a line between the worthy and the unworthy poor. As long as conditions in the poorhouse were sufficiently miserable—that is, "less eligible than any other mode of life"—only the severely destitute would enter. In this way, conditions within the poorhouse itself would serve as a "self-acting test of the claim of the applicant." In other words, "If the claimant does not comply with the terms on which relief is given to the destitute, he gets nothing; and if he does comply, the compliance proves the truth of the claim, namely, his destitution." "Thus the instrument of relief was itself the test for relief."[14]

But what about the worthy poor, those who could not work? Because all outdoor relief had to be abolished to avoid line-drawing, the worthy poor also had to go to the poorhouse. And because the conditions of the poorhouse were to be sufficiently miserable to deter the able-bodied, the worthy poor—who had no other alternative—had to endure misery in order to deter the able-bodied. As Michael Katz puts it, the worthy poor were held "hostage" to deter the able-bodied. In the words of Prime Minister Benjamin Disraeli decades later, the English Poor Law Reform Bill of 1834 made it "a crime to be poor."

In the United States, outdoor relief was also blamed as a prime source of pauperism. Although American reforms were far less draconian and in fact were designed to eliminate some of the harsher practices, such as auctioning off the poor, increased use of the poorhouse was emphasized. Reformers had good reason to be optimistic about poorhouses at first. Towns and cities that had poorhouses in the 1820s reported good results—lower relief costs and improved behavior. According to Katz, these reports were exaggerated; because there was always opposition to poorhouses, they could not have been viewed as benign. Besides, within a few years after the reforms took hold, the reports on the poorhouses documented a disaster. Graft, corruption, and brutality were common; alcohol was smuggled in; inmates came and went; filth and disorder prevailed; criminals, alcoholics, women, mothers, children, and infants were mixed together. Mortality rates were high. Poorhouses were described as "living tombs" and "social cemeteries."[15] Able-bodied inmates were supposed to work, but in many poorhouses it was cheaper to support them in idleness, especially during winter. In many places, work was used as deterrence only. For example, poorhouses would use treadmills rather than horses or, later, steam-driven machinery. In the poorhouse at Providence, Rhode Island, men piled up wood in one corner of the yard and then moved it to another. This practice was justified as ridding the community "of all lazy drones, such as infest our poor houses to a great degree."[16]

In England, the Poor Law of 1834 was generally regarded as a failure. Strong opposition mounted to what quickly became a detested institution. Neighbors protected friends and relatives; local riots broke out; and rural landlords, who wanted a ready supply of cheap labor, complained. Local relief administrators found loopholes and other ways to avoid placing people in poorhouses. One of the most powerful objections to the new Poor Law was the stigma that flowed from the very attempt to distinguish so sharply the pauper from the merely poor. The deprivation of liberty by confinement in the wretched poorhouse—so visible and dramatic a symbol—not only solidified the image of the pauper but tainted the laboring poor, too. Poverty had indeed become a crime. And in spite of the eventual decline of the poorhouse, the stigma lived on.[17]

In the United States, although the number of poorhouses

grew rapidly, the remedy also failed.[18] There was no rehabilitation; needless suffering was great, certainly for those who were not in the labor market but were nevertheless confined; and in the end, institutionalization turned out to be more expensive than outdoor relief.

The reasons for the failure transcend the particular experience of the poorhouse reform. First, poorhouses tried to do two things that eventually proved to be inconsistent. They sought to be compassionate to those who were truly needy—the aged, the sick, children—while having to deter the able-bodied from applying. This meant that the conditions of relief could not be attractive. In the end, as Katz points out, deterrence won, and the poorhouses became universally feared and despised. The truly needy were forced to live in miserable conditions to deter the able-bodied. Second, the reforms focused on the individual poor person; personal fault was the cause of poverty, and moral reformation the cure. No attention was paid to the supply of jobs; it was assumed that work was available for those who had the right attitude.

Outdoor relief continued to grow. In the later nineteenth century, despite severe recessions, governments again attempted to restrict outdoor relief, voicing the usual concerns about the rise of relief, the increase in public costs, the threat to the social order, and the labor supply. The same beliefs were professed: that most of those who were on relief did not need aid; that indiscriminate relief became a way of life; that there ensued a loss of independence and self-respect as well as the spread of vice; and that relief interfered with the proper functioning of the labor market.

This time, outdoor relief was to be replaced by "scientific charity." Although the proposed measures were clothed in new theory, the assumptions as to the causes and cures of poverty remained the same. The task was to keep the poor from starving without breeding a class of paupers who choose to live off the public rather than to work. Once again, the distinction between the two classes of poor was cast in moral terms. Poverty, proclaimed one reformer in 1834, was misfortune, an "unavoidable evil," but pauperism was moral fault—"the consequence of wilful error, of shameful indolence, of vicious habits. It is a misery of human creation, the pernicious work of man, the lamentable consequence of bad principles and morals." And relief to paupers increased "the evil in a tenfold degree." A rise in immigration strengthened the emphasis on moral defect. The alien newcomers, often confined to ghettos, were blamed as one of the largest sources of pauperism.[19]

Private charity was favored over outdoor relief. Charity, it was argued, had several advantages over public assistance. Assistance would not be a right but would be more uncertain, thus not weakening the work ethic. Charities were more resistant to political pressure to liberalize benefits and more effective in exerting "those moral and religious influences that would prevent relief from degenerating into a mechanical pauperizing dole."[20]

The New York Association for Improving the Condition of the Poor (AICP), active in the 1840s, provided an earlier but influential example of the advantages of private charity. This organization had warned that the poor would "over-run the city as thieves and beggars and endanger the security of property and life—tax the community for their support and entail upon it an inheritance of vice and pauperism."[21] The leading causes of poverty, in the AICP's view were extravagance, improvidence, indolence, and, above all, intemperance —all noneconomic factors. Drink was clearly the leading cause of want and woe. The "environmental causes of poverty" were "filth, crime, sexual promiscuity, drunkenness, disease, improvidence, and indolence"—these were the "serious obstacles to morality." In Walter Trattner's view, the AICP "probably loved the poor less than they feared or perhaps even hated them. . . . [T]he A.I.C.P. was no more a charitable agency than an instrument for reducing relief costs and keeping society orderly, stable, and quiet."[22]

Katz points out that—then, as now—the reformers' view of relief recipients was sharply at odds with who actually received outdoor relief. Most recipients were, in fact, widows, children, the aged, and the sick. Very few, he writes, could work. The reformers, however, considered outdoor relief a threat not necessarily because of whom it helped but because of those who *might* be helped. In other words, the very existence of outdoor relief was a threat to the work ethic. The "respectable working class just might learn the possibility of life without labor."[23]

Even though economic dislocation meant a growing need for assistance, scientific charity nevertheless justified assaults on outdoor relief. Echoing Tocqueville and Malthus, and bolstered by Herbert Spencer, reformers wrote that poverty was "the direct consequence of sloth and sinfulness." As another writer put it, "The only solution to poverty is 'nature's remedy—work or starve.'"[24] In spite of the hardships of the 1870s—federal troops had to put down rioting in several large cities—many charity officials strongly opposed the "excess" of relief. "Next to alcohol, and perhaps alongside it, the most pernicious fluid is indiscriminate soup." The new scientific charities, according to Trattner, were in the end patterned after the New York AICP. For Josephine Lowell, founder of the New York Charity Organization Society (COS) and a leader of scientific charity, deprivation was clearly essential to keep the poor at work. Signs reading "NO RELIEF GIVEN HERE" were posted at the Buffalo chapter of the COS. If relief had to be given, it had to be given sparingly, in public institutions, for it "should be surrounded by circumstances that shall repel everyone from accepting it," said Lowell.[25]

The campaign against outdoor relief was a symbolic crusade, one to send the right message. For example, in Brooklyn in the late 1870s, even though relief rolls had increased, expenses had not (grants were cut). Nevertheless, wealthy Republicans trying to oust Democrats fought the campaign as a tax and corruption issue.

In many communities, however, the campaigns were both real and successful. Outdoor relief was either abolished or drastically reduced. As a result, by the end of the century, the number of children placed with agencies or in orphanages had mushroomed. Mothers sought jobs as live-in maids. Husbands went on the road looking for work, and local officials began to complain about the increase in tramps, who were mostly younger men in search of work. As with the Poor Law of 1834 in England, the opposition to abolishing outdoor relief was at the local level. There, the superintendents of the poor faced local resistance to sending friends and neighbors to the poorhouse. Local merchants wanted the relief vouchers for food and coal. Local officials were charged with making the distinction between the truly needy and the unworthy. They knew the residents, but for others, the work test was the discriminator. "For strangers, nothing would certify worthiness as well as the willingness to break stone."[26]

These, then, were the attitudes toward the poor as the United States entered the twentieth century and began to build the current welfare state. For more than five hundred years, the relief of those who could not earn their way had focused on the individual rather than on labor markets or other social conditions. The enduring issue was framed in moral terms—the preservation of the work ethic. "Man" (that is, people) was viewed as essentially slothful by nature and would work only if required. The goal of relief, therefore, was not primarily to relieve misery but rather to preserve the work ethic. Yet, although preservation of the work ethic was the central theme, dependency was complex and multicausal. There was vice, filth, criminality, and, above all, intemperance. Always present in relief efforts was hostility to strangers and immigrants—people who differed from the reformers, not only in habits but in race, ethnicity, and religion. Self-sufficiency, therefore, was not only morally valuable in itself but served other goals of family, socialization, conformity, identity, and citizenship. Those who were clearly not in the labor force would be helped, but here the danger was the difficulty in drawing the line between the truly needy and the malingerer. The conditions of relief had to be sufficiently miserable and stigmatic as to deter the working poor. Relief policy was less to reform the poor—who, for the most part could not work anyway—than to send a message to the working population.

The Development of the American Welfare State

The characteristic feature of the American welfare state is its categorical nature. There are separate, distinct programs for specific categories of the poor—Social Security pensions for retired workers and their survivors; disability payments for those who are permanently disabled; AFDC for single mothers and their children;[27] Unemployment Insurance; Workers' Compensation; Medicare for Social Security pensioners; Medicaid for the poor; and General Assistance for the residuals—those who do not fit the other categories—essentially, childless adults under age sixty-five.

The American welfare state is usually dated from the Social Security Act of 1935. That act established a national retirement system, but it also continued and hardened the categorical programs that were enacted in most states between 1910 and the 1920s. In fact, the categories of the American welfare state had their roots in preceding centuries. The early nineteenth-century institutional movement was the start of categorization in the United States. Inheriting the English system, the states dealt with the general mass of the poor—both the worthy and the unworthy—at the local level. About the 1830s, the states began to separate those categories of the poor who were morally blameless—that is, for whom the work ethic was not at issue—and provided separate institutions for the blind, the deaf and mute, and the insane. Later, children were removed from the poorhouses and placed in orphanages. The institutional movement was not a matter of custodial efficiency; rather, it was a clear recognition that those who were dependent by misfortune did not deserve the stigma of the unworthy poor.

The Civil War resulted in a further categorization. The states created separate institutions for Civil War orphans and separate relief programs for indigent veterans and their families. The major program of that era was the Civil War pension program, which, by the end of the century, grew into a massive national income-maintenance system. Indigent veterans were morally excused from work—needy soldiers were not a "class of professional paupers, but are poor by misfortune."[28] In 1910, the program was terminated amid charges of extravagance, corruption, and partisan politics.

At the close of the nineteenth century, then, and just before the enactment of the present categories, the great mass of the poor were helped, if at all, through outdoor relief at the local level. At this time, single mothers and their children were in a difficult position. In practice, they were not differentiated from the general poor. They were not considered to be outside the labor market. They were part of the "unworthy poor." From time to time, they, along with the rest, were helped, but mostly under the most severe conditions. Mothers had to work, and when they could not support their families, their children were placed in orphanages.[29]

Poor, single women, including single mothers, carried the stigma of pauper. But they carried additional burdens, too; in addition to the suspicions of vice, immorality, and intemperance, they threatened patriarchal conceptions of "proper" women and mothers.[30] Under the patriarchal "domestic code," proper women stayed at home and cared for their husbands and children. Along with the myth of the availability of work went the myth of the "family wage"—any hard-working husband could earn an amount sufficient to support the family.[31] Husbands alone were supposed to provide for the material well-being of their families. Proper wives and mothers were not suited to the rough, vulgar world of commerce and paid labor; rather, they were to nurture husbands and children.

Notions of what was considered "proper" defined the deviant. Single women who entered the paid labor force were suspect, often forfeiting marriage. Of course, poor women, whether alone or married, with or without children, had to work, sometimes in the regular labor force, but often in the informal economy. Thus, poor mothers and their children were in a double bind. They were considered to be in the labor market. They were part of the undeserving poor, which meant that they had to work in the paid labor force. Mothers took in laundry, had boarders, were domestics, and, if lucky, worked in factories. Their children also worked. But the families were condemned for working. This was a deviant class.[32] Immigrants and women of color bore additional burdens of discrimination. European immigrants were considered a different race, threatening the United

States unless they became "educated, self-controlled, disciplined." Blacks and Latinos scarcely figured in the social conscience.[33] As Linda Gordon puts it, to be a poor, single African American mother was to be all but an outcast.[34]

In the later nineteenth century, poor children began to be distinguished as a separate category that deserved attention. It was the children of these women—poor, immigrant, minority, working, often alone—that the Child Savers of the Progressive Era were concerned about. The Child Savers was a loose coalition of various social reformers who were unified by the pressing needs of children of the time. Fearing threats posed to middle-class Protestant America by urban slum children, especially in major Northeastern cities, the Child Savers asserted public social control over these families by expanding the concept of neglect. Through child protection laws and the newly created juvenile courts, poor children were removed from their mothers and sent to institutions or farms in the Midwest. The Child Savers claimed that children were never removed for poverty alone, but poverty was never alone. There were always other factors.[35]

Then, around the turn of the century, the idea began to develop among some of the Child Savers that if the problem with children was, in fact, only poverty—that is, if the mother was otherwise fit and proper—then perhaps a solution would be to support the mother rather than break up the home. This idea was endorsed in a White House conference in 1909, and in 1911, the first Aid to Dependent Children (ADC) statute was enacted—the Illinois Fund to Parents Act. The idea spread rapidly; by 1925, similar statutes had been enacted in almost all the states.[36] At the time of these enactments, ADC was popularly known as "mothers' pensions," although most statutes simply used "aid to dependent children."[37]

To understand the significance of the initial ADC programs—what they purported to do and did not do—it is essential to consider the moral context of that time. This was the moment of the full flowering of the patriarchal domestic code. Progressive social reformers—mostly upper-class women—were fully committed to the concepts of the domestic code and the family wage.[38] Those who opposed ADC—and they included many of the most prominent social reformers, also from the upper class—feared that aid to single mothers threatened these same concepts, that aid would weaken the responsibility of fathers and encourage single parenthood. Accordingly, they felt that aid should be given only to "children of worthy character, suffering from temporary misfortune, and children of reasonably efficient and deserving mothers."[39]

The apparent popularity of ADC has since led some observers to regard the mothers' pension movement as a turning point in American social welfare history: poor mothers of young children could now stay at home; they were morally excused from work; they were the "deserving poor"; they were no longer in conflict with the domestic code.[40] Yet, when one looks more closely at what these statutes said and what was actually practiced, aiding single mothers was still morally problematic. The indiscriminate giving of aid continued to raise great concern, especially among the most prominent social reformers. The most influential organization, the Charitable Organization Society, vigorously opposed all forms of outdoor relief, including ADC—recall Josephine Lowell and the Buffalo COS. The statutes only considered single mothers—intact families were excluded. This made no sense if poverty alone was the deciding factor. The reasons for excluding husbands and fathers were that public relief would encourage idleness and lack of responsibility to the family and compromise the moral socialization role of the working male.[41]

There were other restrictions. Aid would be given only if the mother was "fit and proper." Single mothers were by definition suspicious; aid would encourage separation, further weaken the role of husbands and fathers, and increase the vulnerability of the mothers and children to temptation. The statutes did not define "fit and proper"—that job was left to local administrators. In most jurisdictions, relief was administered not by the welfare department but the juvenile and county court—the courts that could, in addition to giving aid, adjudicate children delinquent, dependent, or neglected, break up homes, and incarcerate children in either reformatories or state schools. Assisting the courts in many jurisdictions were the local COS chapters; they would ensure that aid would not contribute to vice. Programs were means tested and "morals tested" and supervised to ensure that mothers learned the proper work habits and morals that the reformers thought they lacked. In most jurisdictions, ADC mothers could be required to work. By locating the programs in the courts and by having such organizations as local COS chapters supervise the recipients, ADC was, in effect, an alternative form of probation.

From its earliest days, then, ADC was an exercise in myth and ceremony. The myth was that poor mothers would be allowed to stay at home and take care of their children—hence the popular name "mothers' pensions." The ceremony was that a small number of deserving white widows were helped; this validated the myth. The reality was that, for most poor, single mothers and their children, at best, nothing had changed; at worst, they were stigmatized further by being excluded from the mothers' pension programs.[42] In practice, ADC programs remained small. Relatively few families were enrolled; recipients were almost exclusively white widows; grants were small; even these mothers had work requirements. Excluded outright were most poor mothers—those who were divorced, deserted, never married, of color, or engaged in questionable behavior. In short, the myth was that poor mothers and children were now the deserving poor. The reality was that the vast majority of poor mothers and their children were still morally problematic; they were still considered part of the paid labor force; they were denied aid. They were the undeserving poor.

Programs to aid the blind were enacted at about the same time as ADC, but the contrast between the two was striking. Blindness was a "sufficiently well-defined cause of poverty"; the blind, therefore, were the deserving poor. Eligibility was clear-cut—in addition to blindness, factors were age, residence, and need. In some states, the only moral condition was that the applicant not be a beggar. In contrast to ADC legislation, which was usually part of the juvenile code, statues to aid to the blind were administered by welfare departments, not juvenile or county courts.

Old-Age Assistance (OAA) was introduced in the 1920s, but in contrast to the blind, OAA more closely resembled ADC. At this time—before the Depression—no retirement age had been agreed upon, and the aged poor were viewed with as much suspicion as other poor people. Aid to the aged poor, it was thought, would threaten the values of hard work and saving and family responsibility. Not only were OAA programs hard to enact, but, like ADC, they were small, uneven in coverage, and filled with provisions designed to weed out the unworthy—in many states, for example, aid would be denied persons who had deserted their spouses or failed to support them, had been convicted of crimes, or were "habitual tramps, vagrants, or beggars."[43]

Workers' Compensation, another important social reform, had yet a different legal and administrative structure. By the beginning of the twentieth century, prominent capitalists, organized labor, and social reformers began to express alarm at the rise and costs of industrial accidents, primarily from steel, railroads, and mines. Traditional common law defenses began to crumble under pressure of public outrage and increasing negative publicity about the uncompensated losses suffered by working people. To stabilize costs and avoid increasingly unpredictable common law tort recoveries, employers pushed through an administrative compensation scheme whereby employees would receive benefits according to fixed tables for calculating the extent of a disability, wage replacement, and medical expenses. Programs were administered through separate agencies; with few exceptions, employees lost the right to sue. Employees still bore most of the costs of injuries.[44]

This was the pattern on the eve of the New Deal. When consensus forms on the nature of a social problem and its solutions, then program design is transparent and ideologically consistent. This is true whether programs are benign, such as separate state institutions, veterans' pensions, and aid to the blind, or repressive, such as workers' compensation. Conversely, when moral responsibility is at issue, ambiguity and conflict follow. Here, programs are delegated to the local level and decided on a case-by-case basis. Aid to single mothers and their children, old-age assistance, and general relief to the undifferentiated able-bodied raises issues of work, responsibility, race, gender roles, moral behavior, and child protection.

The Roosevelt administration was absorbed with funding retirement and the unemployed. It cared little for welfare. The centerpiece of the Social Security Act was the establishment of a contributory national pension program for the retired worker—Old Age Insurance (OAI), popularly known as Social Security. For a variety of reasons, the country did settle on a retirement age, and people over sixty-five were now excused from work. Contributory insurance meant protection for clearly defined "risks." There would be no means test, so that beneficiaries would not have the stigma of the dependent poor. The Roosevelt administration fought vigorously and successfully to compensate only workers who contributed and to exclude the poor aged lest the program be considered "welfare." In short, Social Security was for the deserving worker, and it remained relatively small until after World War II, when most of the aged poor were finally blanketed in. OAI was a national, uniform program administered by the Social Security Administration.

The biggest fight that the administration had was over Unemployment Insurance (UI), or, more particularly, the *jurisdictional location* of UI. Unemployment, especially on the massive scale of the Depression, would logically appear to have been a national problem requiring national solutions. But the unemployed were different from the aged. For here was involved not only the work ethic but race. In the end, race relations and business control over local labor markets prevailed. UI was handled at the state and local levels. At the local level, programs failed to reach those most in need—employees of small firms, agricultural workers, women, African Americans, migrants. State benefits were low and short-term, more in the nature of temporary emergency relief. State laws incorporated a variety of eligibility provisions to ensure that benefits were paid only to deserving workers—that is, workers who had been steady and reliable in covered employment. Workers who quit or were fired or discharged because of a labor dispute or who failed to register at a public employment agency and be available for suitable work were not eligible.

ADC, along with OAA and Aid to the Blind, became a grant-in-aid. There were a few federal requirements, but basically state and local governments administered the program as they saw fit. And until about the early 1960s, ADC remained small, and still basically for white widows. Because there were no other welfare programs (except very uneven and miserly local general relief), poor mothers and their children had to work or otherwise obtain money as best they could. That is, despite ADC, the vast majority of poor, single mothers and their children—mothers who were separated, divorced, or never married, or who were of color—were treated no differently than the other categories of undeserving poor; relief was denied and they were subject to the paid labor market.[45]

Dramatic changes came in the late 1950s and 1960s. Racial tensions flared into urban riots as large numbers of African Americans moved north seeking civil rights and industrial jobs in the northern cities. The Democratic Party courted urban African Americans, and, along with the civil rights revolution, there was a legal rights revolution. The federal courts and welfare rights activists forced open the ADC gates. Welfare became a "right," and in streamed the previously excluded—women of color, divorced, separated, deserted, and, increasingly, never-married.[46] Were these previously excluded, morally problematic recipients now to be treated as the deserving poor and excused from work? Not so. Welfare was now in "crisis." Although some punitive, moralistic eligibility restrictions were struck down, starting in 1967 and continuing through the Family Support Act of 1988, federal and state work requirements were applied to able-bodied welfare mothers.

Liberals vigorously fought the work requirements, arguing that if nonwelfare mothers were not required to work, then it was unfair and punitive to impose work requirements on single poor mothers. Conservatives thought otherwise. In their view, single poor mothers did not shed their historical undeserving status simply because misguided liberals let them into AFDC. They differed morally from mothers who were either man-dependent or self-sufficient, and so they should be required to work.

For the next twenty years, a standoff ensued. As I discuss in chapter 4, the work requirements never worked in the sense of reducing rolls through employment, setting the poor to work, or imposing sanctions for failure to comply. Most welfare recipients were either declared ineligible for the programs or otherwise excused from the requirements. Just as with the earliest mothers' pensions, the country collectively engaged in myth and ceremony. The myth was that Americans were going to reduce welfare by imposing the moral values of work; the ceremony was the small number of recipients that did leave welfare through employment (whether as a result of the work programs is another matter); and meanwhile, the vast majority of welfare recipients continued to be condemned for their dependency. They were still the undeserving poor.

Both sides remained unhappy. Conservatives continued to attack the "entitlement state" on the grounds that there are *responsibilities* as well as rights in the social contract. Then, in the late 1980s, a strange thing happened. The liberals changed. Instead of arguing that it was unfair to require AFDC mothers to work, they now maintained that AFDC mothers should be *expected* to work. Two reasons were given. First, social norms concerning female labor have changed. The majority of nonwelfare mothers, including mothers of young children, are now in the paid labor force, and it is therefore reasonable to expect welfare mothers to work. Second, families are better off, both materially and socially, when the adults are gainfully employed. It is bad (morally) when families are continually dependent.[47] Liberals supported the state work demonstration projects and the Job Opportunities and Basic Skills Training Program (JOBS), created by the Family Support Act of 1988.[48]

Conservatives have had a consistent agenda for about six centuries—poor mothers and their children are the undeserving poor, and the adults, at least, should be set to work. In a sense, liberals have also been consistent. Poor mothers should be treated the same as mothers who are not poor. From the first ADC programs until the 1980s, liberals argued that under the domestic code, mothers are not expected to work in the paid labor force. Now they still want to treat welfare mothers the same as nonwelfare mothers. All are expected to work.

As is customary in American politics, the current proposals designed to enforce work by limiting welfare are being hailed as new when in fact they are painfully old. As we have seen, they perpetuate false beliefs about the causes and remedies of poverty that are now almost 650 years old.

This brief review of the history of welfare shows two things: (1) poor mothers, including those on welfare, have *always* been required to work—it is a myth to think that *new* "responsibilities" are now being asked; and (2) although contemporary welfare policies are often described in so-called objective terms—labor markets, wage rates, incentives, demographics—they are heavily laden with moral judgments. Who the poor are, whether they should be helped, and under what circumstances are social processes that affirm moral norms of work, family, gender roles, and attitudes toward race and ethnicity.

Conservatives are right in arguing that work is a moral responsibility. Personal identity is defined in terms of work. "If you're out of work, you're nobody," is endlessly repeated by the unemployed. Working parents are proper role models for children. Those who without socially approved excuses fail to support themselves and their families through paid labor are "bums" and "malingerers." Yet, the aged, children, and the unambiguously disabled are excused from work. They are the "deserving" poor. The idle rich are more envied than admired; approval is reserved for those who do service.

Accordingly, whether and how to help those who cannot support themselves is a moral judgment. Characteristics of welfare programs vary with the *beliefs* as to the *reasons* for poverty. If the claimants are considered to be morally excused from the labor market, then society historically has been relatively forthcoming. Welfare for the blind, the deaf, and Civil War orphans and veterans came relatively early and was generous for the time. Once as a society Americans agreed on a retirement age, a national pension program was established that compares favorably by industrial world standards.[49]

When the reasons for poverty are morally ambiguous, programs are less generous and more suspicious. When able-bodied people are unemployed, we worry why they are unemployed and whether aid will discourage them from trying harder. We try to restrict benefits to the "deserving" worker—those who have worked steadily, were involuntarily laid off, and are actively seeking work; after a relatively short time, benefits stop.[50] Disability, too, can be morally ambiguous when the impairment is not readily observable. We work, we are taught, because it is our duty, not because it is necessarily pleasant. Is the disability claimant "really" disabled or just "unhappy" about working?[51] At the bottom of the scale are the able-bodied poor, who lack all socially approved excuses. These are primarily childless adults below retirement age. In many parts of the United States, these people are either not helped at all or receive benefits through programs (General Relief) that are short-term, miserly, and have stiff work requirements. The work ethic is enforced through deterrence.

Aid to single mothers and their children has always been morally problematic. Although women and mothers in general were not considered part of the paid labor force until recent decades, this has never been true for poor women and mothers. They had to work, even though they were condemned for it. Today they are still considered part of the labor force but are condemned for their failure to attain self-sufficiency. Accordingly, AFDC, as a program for the undeserving poor, is locally based, regulatory, and miserly. Its domain is moral behavior.

3 The Problem of Poverty, the Problem of Work

The contemporary consensus on work as the solution to welfare dependency was formed when the liberals switched positions recently. Liberals have consistently argued that welfare mothers should be treated the same as nonwelfare mothers, and now that the majority of nonwelfare mothers are in the paid labor force, they argue that it is reasonable to expect welfare mothers to do the same.

There are a number of problems with the new liberal position. First, nonwelfare mothers work by choice and can choose to be man-dependent; although this may seem a little curious today, there is no stigma or sanction. Welfare recipients do not have this choice. Second, we know from twenty-five years' experience that setting the poor to work is expensive and extremely problematic administratively; this should give us pause before we embrace another "new solution." Third, given child care problems, health care issues, school problems, bad neighborhoods, and so forth, it is questionable how young children and adolescents will fare when their mothers have to work enough hours to achieve self-sufficiency. As with nonwelfare mothers, these decisions should be left to the individual families. Related, and fourth, perhaps we ought to rethink the value of mother-provided child care and concentrate on better ways of supporting families so that they can make decisions based on their needs.

Although I think that these are important arguments and will return to them shortly, I wish to make a different one. The way the debate is framed—"welfare" as contrasted with "work"—is obsolete and counterproductive. It is the same argument used for the Statute of Laborers. The argument did not work then, and it will not work now. It no longer applies to either the present or the future, and as long as we continue to think in these terms, we not only will fail to develop more effective policies but will repeat the myths and ceremonies and moral condemnation of welfare history.

The Problem of Poverty

Concerns about welfare dependency cluster around two issues—family values and the work ethic. Included in discussions of family values are concerns that men aren't supporting mothers and children; mothers aren't marrying; and children aren't cared for—they suffer from ill health, poor nutrition, bad parenting, and dangerous neighborhoods. Children growing up in these families fail to make successful transitions to adulthood, and the cycle is repeated. The standard euphemism is "counter-culture poverty." The image, often unspoken, is the black ghetto "underclass."

These concerns are real. Large numbers of children and youth are suffering and are at great risk of not becoming successful adults.[1] But the root problem is poverty, and this is much larger than welfare. To discuss this, we need some numbers. The most convenient way to talk about poverty is to use the federal poverty line. The poverty line, established in 1955, is calculated on what a family would need to spend on a minimally adequate diet and then multiplied by three. It was, and is, an austere budget. The dollar amount is adjusted for inflation but does not include noncash benefits, such as food stamps, housing subsidies, and Medicaid. In 1993, the poverty line for a family of four was $14,763.

The federal poverty line is controversial. Conservatives argue that noncash benefits ought to be included, thus lowering the line; liberals claim that housing costs now take a far larger share of a family's budget and that the line should be raised. Although it is still convenient to use the official line—which will be used here—it must be recognized that it is very low. Most Americans, according to a Gallup poll conducted in 1989, think that a family of three needs about $16,000 a year to get by.[2]

According to the official poverty line, more than 39 million Americans live in poverty. In 1989, moreover, 38 percent of the poor, or 14 million Americans, reported income of less than *one-half* the poverty line.[3] Now, it is true that this is *reported* income, but still, 14 million people are very poor. The poverty line is an arbitrary cut-off; by definition, it excludes millions of people whose incomes are technically above the line but who nevertheless live on the margin—the "near poor." They lack education and training and work at insecure jobs without health insurance or other benefits. There is insufficient quality day care. At about 150 percent of the poverty line, roughly $21,000 for a family of four, there are more than 30 million people, including 6 million full-time and 5.5 million part-time workers. "At this income level there is barely enough for the lowest-cost necessities such as food, housing, clothing, transportation, and medical care, and nothing at all for what better-off Americans take for granted—meals out, vacations, child care, lessons or allowances for children, haircuts, and so on."[4]

Whatever figures one uses—the near poor or the official poor—the welfare population is considerably smaller. The number of people on welfare in 1993 stood at 13.6 million. This is a lot of people, but it is only about a third of the poverty population. Another way of looking at relative size is to consider child poverty. The 13.6 million on welfare includes 9.2 million children. But almost 22 percent of all children, or 14.3 million, are living in families below the poverty line, and this is an increase of nearly 1 million since 1990.[5]

The reason for these large and increasing numbers of poor people is that family income has deteriorated significantly. Between 1973 and 1990, the median income declined almost a third for families headed by parents under age thirty. Although the problem is most acute for single-parent families, most two-parent families have been able to maintain their relative position only if both parents work. In fact, there is a growing trend for one of these two earners to now hold two jobs. Seven million Americans, or 6 percent of the work force, hold 15 million jobs. Most multiple job holders are married, and, increasingly, as many of them are women as are men. No other country approaches these numbers of multiple jobholders. The reason, according to Richard Freeman, is that wages from one job are sufficient in other countries.[6] Today, the majority (61 percent) of children have mothers who are in the paid labor force; moreover, these mothers are working longer hours—over 30 percent more than a decade ago.[7]

Family structure has changed dramatically during the past two decades. Although most children still live in two-parent families, the number of single-parent households, mostly female-headed, has grown significantly, and they now account for about 25 percent of all children. Single-parent households are much more likely to be poor than two-parent households. Although female-headed households represent about 10 percent of the population, they account for more than a third of the poverty population and more than half of the increase in poverty since 1990.[8] Almost three-quarters of all children in single-parent households will experience at least some poverty while they are growing up. For African American children, the poverty spell will be extended. Because almost all of these single parents are women, gender discrimination limits their ability to earn a living. In spite of women's participation in the labor market, the economic circumstances of a family decline after divorce primarily because of a lack of child support. It is thus no surprise that "single parents are twice as likely as married couples to be worried about 'making ends meet' and concerned that their children will 'get beat up,' 'get pregnant,' 'not get a job,' or 'drop out of school.'"[9]

Two-parent households will not necessarily escape poverty. In most poor households, there is only partial employment or unemployment, but even in families with two wage earners, a fifth remain poor. In these poor households, fewer than half of the unemployed workers receive unemployment compensation, and jobs found after unemployment usually pay, on average, about a third less than previous jobs. David Ellwood thinks that because many of the full-time working poor families fail to qualify for benefits, such as Medicaid, they may be actually the poorest of the poor.[10]

Although low income is not the exclusive cause of family behavior, the fact remains that poverty is the most powerful predictor of the harmful behavioral consequences we ascribe to welfare families. As Sara McLanahan and Gary Sandefur state, "Low income or income loss is the single most important factor in accounting for the lower achievement of children in single-parent families. It accounts for half of the difference in educational achievement, weak labor force attachment, and early childbearing."[11] Not surprisingly, parents in these families suffer more emotionally and are more anxious about their children's future than better-off parents. Poor families are more likely to disintegrate and become single-parent households, and single-parents, in turn, are less likely to engage in "good" parenting practices. Even allowing for the problems of official reporting, the highest incidence of child neglect and abuse and the most severe injuries to children occur in the poorest families. Economic instability and hardship and social stress among adults is related to marital conflict and harsh and inconsistent punishment, rejection, and noninvolvement. Brain dysfunctions, caused by exposure to lead, injuries from abuse, or mothers' substance abuse—all highly correlated with poverty—interfere with language and cognitive development, resulting in learning and social problems at school. Early school failure, in turn, is one of the strongest predictors of adolescent problems, including violent behavior. It is not surprising that children growing up in poor families are more likely to suffer from poor physical and mental health problems, do poorly at school, and compromise successful development by early sex, pregnancy, substance abuse, delinquency, and crime.

Education is a crucial determinant of future employment, and low income (income less than 150 percent of the poverty line) seriously affects educational achievement. Poor children attend schools of inferior quality; they cannot afford after-school enrichment activities; and their parents are both likely to have lower expectations and less likely to be involved with their schooling and to invest in themselves.[12] When income is controlled, school dropout rates are fairly similar regardless of race.[13] Approximately the same percentages of white, black, and Latino students will have neither a high school diploma nor a general equivalency diploma by the time they reach twenty-four. And people without a high school degree or its equivalent are severely disadvantaged in an already difficult job market.

Because there is such a high correlation between poverty and single-parent households, it is hard to separate out the effects of each disadvantage. It's a case of double jeopardy, for both the parents and the children. As Uri Bronfenbrenner summarizes it,

> The developmental risks associated with a one-parent family structure are relatively small . . . in comparison with those involved in two other types of environmental contexts. The first and most destructive of these is poverty. Because many single-parent families are also poor, parents and their children are in double jeopardy. But even when two parents are present, . . . in households living under stressful economic and social conditions, processes of parent-child interaction and environmentally oriented child activity are more difficult to initiate and sustain.
>
> To be sure, . . . when the mother, or some other adult committed to the child's well-being, does manage to establish and maintain a pattern of progressive reciprocal interaction, the disruptive impact of poverty on development

is significantly reduced. But, among the poor, the proportion of parents who, despite their stressful life circumstances, are able to provide quality care is, under present circumstances, not very large. And even for this minority, the parents' buffering power begins to decline sharply by the time children are five or six years old and exposed to impoverished and disruptive settings outside the home.[14]

One important risk for adolescent deviant behavior is parents leaving kids alone. Understandably, overloaded single parents are more likely to give their children more autonomy.[15] It is estimated that the average parent spends eleven fewer hours per week with his or her children than in 1960; less than 5 percent of families have another adult, such as a grandparent, living in the house to relieve the burden. As a result, children are increasingly on their own. The National Commission on Children estimated in 1991 that 1.3 million children aged five to fourteen are on their own after school.[16] This is important to bear in mind when employment and work requirements are being discussed.

The risk of a poor outcome is increased when the parent is a teenager. The children of these parents are even more likely to do poorly in school and to engage in compromising behaviors. Again, it is hard to separate the effects of teen parenting from low income. There are some differences between white and black teenage mothers. Whereas white teenage mothers are more likely to marry, black teenage mothers are more likely to live in an extended household. Although black teenage mothers stay longer on welfare, they are also more likely to graduate from high school.[17]

A recent synthesis of research on adolescents at risk conducted by a panel of the National Research Council concluded:

> The combination of financial insecurity for an increasing proportion of families, increased work effort by parents seeking to maintain their living standard, and the demographic changes that have so dramatically increased the number of

children and adolescents living in single-parent households result in increasing numbers of adolescents who do not receive the nurturance necessary for positive development. The consequences are not inescapably negative. Indeed, the majority of adolescents—even those from poor and single-parent homes—do succeed despite the obstacles. However, the adverse outcomes—the failure rates—are unacceptably and unnecessarily high.[18]

The problems attributed to welfare are, in reality, the problems of poverty. Large numbers of parents are working, yet not escaping poverty. This is especially true for the growing number of single parents. Why is this happening, and what implications does this have for moving single mothers from welfare to work?

The Problem of Work

If the problem is poverty, and the vast majority of the poor are working and not on welfare, then what is the problem of work? Several studies on the growing inequality of earnings have all reached a similar conclusion—namely, that the real earnings of the less skilled, less educated workers have declined substantially since 1973.[19] This decline, moreover, occurred during a period of economic expansion and aggregate growth in employment. In 1973, men with one to three years of high school had a median income of $24,079 (in 1989 dollars); in 1989, the median was $14,439. Men with a high school diploma saw income drop from $30,252 to $21,650. In 1973, women with one to three years of high school had a median income of $7,920; by 1989, the median was $6,752. Women with a high school degree had a median income of $11,087 in 1973 and $10,439 in 1989.[20] Furthermore, the decline in income was not because of the shift in jobs from manufacturing to service; real wages declined in both sectors.

Overall, wages for less skilled women have not declined as men's wages. The primary reason, according to Rebecca Blank, is that less skilled women are in occupations and industries that have not suffered such severe wage declines. However, although men's and women's wages are now closer, women still earn substantially less. For example, women who have not graduated from high school earn less than 60 percent of similarly situated men.[21]

With the decline in real wages, the poverty rate of full-time workers is increasing. According to the latest figures, in 1992, 18 percent of full-time workers earned less than the poverty line, which is a 50 percent increase over the past thirteen years. The poverty rate of full-time workers increased for both men and women but was particularly steep for those without a high school degree. For men without a high school degree, the poverty rate rose from 15 percent in 1979 to 32 percent in 1992—and this is for full-time workers.[22] It is not surprising that over the past two decades, there has been a steady decline in work among men in families in the bottom fifth of the income distribution (earning less than $12,497 in 1989).[23] Although the expansion of low-wage (below poverty-level) jobs affected all workers, it was greatest for minorities. Between 1979 and 1987, the proportion of African Americans in these jobs increased from 33.9 to 40.6 percent, for Latinos from 31.7 to 42.1 percent, and for whites from 24.3 to 29.3 percent.[24]

Not only have earnings declined, but so has employment for both high school graduates and dropouts. Although the unemployment rate for all workers was roughly the same in 1974 as it was in 1988, it doubled for these two groups. It is this combination—declining real earnings and rising unemployment—that has resulted in increasing poverty among these young families. They simply cannot work their way out of poverty.

The low-income employment rates of married women increased over these two decades. It is important to note, however, that higher proportions of single women, even with children, work more than married women, with or without children. Almost half (48.3 percent) of poor, single mothers work, as compared to 29.8 percent of married women without children and 39.9 percent with children. But the most important point is that earnings for these groups has fallen because real wages have declined.[25]

The future does not look good for the less-skilled worker.

First, sectoral shifts in employment have meant a decline in manufacturing opportunities for this group. Wages in the service sector are lower, but skill levels are higher. Second, although unemployment rates in general have stabilized, younger, less educated, and especially black workers are the last to be hired and the first to be fired. For both men and women, unemployment rates are considerably higher for people of color than for whites. Third, although the impact of immigration varies throughout the nation, there has been a large overall increase in less-educated immigrants, which has contributed to the shrinking labor market for high school dropouts.[26]

A decline in union membership has meant a loss of higher wage jobs. The minimum wage has declined significantly in real terms.[27] At $4.25 per hour (the rate in 1995), a full-time worker supporting a family of four has earnings that are only two-thirds of the poverty line. Almost 5 million workers are stuck in minimum-wage jobs.

Other factors contributing to the bleak picture for the less skilled worker include what is called the "spacial mismatch"—the fact that jobs continue to leave the inner cities for the suburbs. There continues to be discrimination against men and women of color. Empirical research has shown strong prejudices against African Americans who are associated with the culture of the inner cities.[28]

On the supply side, it is often argued that a decline in basic reading and math skills accounts for the decreased earnings of the less educated. Yet earnings for African Americans fell while their test scores and academic achievement rose, and earnings of less educated cohorts fell as they aged. The more likely explanation is that academic skills have not kept pace with job requirements.[29]

Crime, of course, affects employment. It not only provides an attractive alternative for the less educated, especially in the drug trade, but is also a disqualification for legitimate employment. In any event, as we know, the number of young, less educated, especially African American males who are involved in the criminal justice system is staggering.[30]

Continued levels of unemployment exacerbate the problems

of the less educated worker. Of the workers who lost their jobs in 1988, 78 percent were reemployed by 1990. However, 60 percent had been jobless for five or more weeks, almost 10 percent were still unemployed, and just over 12 percent were no longer in the work force. Many displaced workers suffered earnings losses when they were rehired. A worker's likelihood of being employed depended on the length of time with the previous employer, number of years of school completed, age, gender, and the local unemployment rate. High school dropouts, older workers, women, and minorities were less likely to be reemployed.[31]

Earnings opportunities are seriously affected by household composition. In 1960, about a quarter of female-headed families were poor; now it is more than half (53 percent in 1992). These families are poor because there is typically only one earner, they usually have child care expenses, and women earn less than men, even when they work the same number of hours.[32]

Not only is there the spread of low-wage jobs, but the nature of employment is shifting from full-time work for a single employer to various forms of "contingent" work.[33] Many workers are employed in part-time, temporary, contract, or other types of flexible work arrangements that lack job security. The General Accounting Office estimated that in 1988 there were 32 million contingent workers, accounting for almost a quarter of the work force. The contingent work force grew rapidly in the 1980s and is expected to increase again because new jobs are expected to be almost entirely in the service sector, where contingent employment is most likely to occur. According to the Bureau of Labor Statistics, almost two-thirds of new entrants into the labor force by the year 2000 will be women, and they are more likely than men to hold part-time and temporary jobs. Although most part-time workers are women, men now account for a significant fraction.[34] It is estimated that by the turn of the century, 40 percent of jobs could be part-time.[35]

Part-time work has both positive and negative aspects. At its worst, it is a disguised form of unemployment. It can be good for some workers: it provides additional income, flexible hours, and continued attachment to the labor force for those workers who pursue other activities. With the rapid growth of nontraditional families, many workers are interested in part-time work. This would be true for both single parents and two-earner families with children. In any event, in the 1980s, *involuntary* part-time work grew 13 percent, but 45 percent during the 1980–83 recession.[36] In contrast, voluntary part-time work grew by 19 percent during the decade. More than three-quarters of part-time workers say that they voluntarily choose this status. It is not clear what "voluntary" means as measured by the Bureau of Labor Statistics. The data do not reveal why part-time workers look only for part-time work—for example, child care, transportation, and health costs may operate as constraints. Further, if female heads of households are more constrained than male heads to work part-time, income inequality (and poverty) will increase as the sex distribution of family heads continues to change.[37]

More than a quarter of women work part-time, making them one and a half times more likely to be so employed than the average worker. "While women are more likely to *choose* part-time work, they are also more likely to be *stuck* in part-time jobs against their will. The female rate of involuntary part-time work is 44 percent greater than that for men."[38] In any event, the real growth in part-time employment has been in involuntary part-time jobs, indicating that employer, not employee, preferences are predominating.[39]

Part-time jobs are more likely to be dead-end. Part-time workers keep their jobs for shorter periods than full-time workers. The average job tenure for a part-time worker is 3.4 years, as compared to 5.7 years for full-time working women and 8.1 years for full-time working men. Not only do part-time workers often lack health and pension benefits, but they also receive a lower hourly wage. Controlling for education, gender, and age, part-time workers receive about 40 percent less per hour than full-time workers in the same jobs. Part-time workers are disproportionately in the low-wage distribution, and these workers constitute 65 percent of all people working at or below minimum wage.[40] As a result, families headed by part-time workers are four times more likely to be below the poverty line as compared to families headed by full-time workers. A fifth of families headed by part-time workers are in poverty, and 12 percent also received welfare, as compared to 2 percent of families headed by full-time workers. Again, single-parent families were worse off—40 percent of these families were poor, and 26 percent were on welfare.[41]

The significant portion of employees in part-time work, and the expected proportional growth of this form of employment, indicate that underemployment will continue to be a concern. Hugh Heclo sums up the effect of low-wages and poverty:

> In 1990, of the 2 million married couples with children living below the official poverty line, 63 percent of the adults were working at least some of the year, and over a third had work levels approaching the equivalent of full-time work all year. Likewise, half of the 3.7 million poor, single mothers with children worked some of the year, and almost a fifth were in, or close to, full-time, full-year employment. . . . If anything, the adults in such poor families with children were working more in 1990 than in 1975. To define the poverty problem as simply a matter of unmotivated, unfunctional people who need government's tough love to make them seize the opportunities surrounding them is absurd.[42]

This, then, is the labor market for the population we are concerned with—the less educated mother of young children, disproportionately of color: overall declining real wages, increasing education and skill requirements (even more than high school) for the better jobs, and increasing low-wage, part-time jobs without benefits. How does the welfare population match the labor market?

The Welfare Population

The popular stereotype or myth is that welfare is composed primarily of young black women who have lots of children, are long-term dependent, and pass on this dependency from generation to generation. On examination, we find that most welfare recipients are not African American; that few are teenagers, especially young teenagers; that welfare families have about the same number of children or fewer than nonwelfare families; that most are on welfare for relatively short periods; but that most remain quite poor, and this probably accounts for their children being more likely to have welfare spells when they are older as compared to children whose parents did not experience welfare. When we then examine how welfare recipients survive, we find that a great many are most likely already working. They may be working off the books, but they are working. And most work their way off welfare.

In 1993, the total AFDC bill for assistance payments was $22.3 billion; the federal share was $12.2 billion.[43] Although this is not a trivial amount, it is well to keep in mind that AFDC is a small program, in terms of both recipients and budget dollars. The federal Food Stamps program, for example, is twice as big—26.6 million people (10.4 percent of the U.S. population), costing $23 billion in

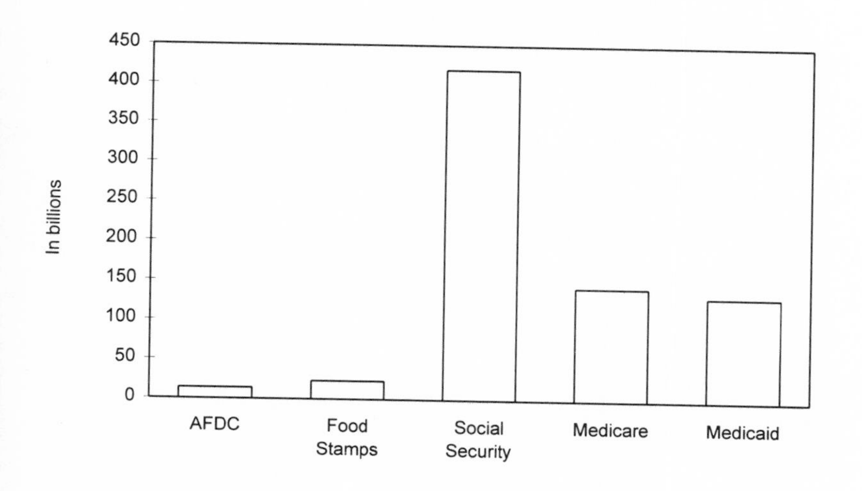

Figure 1 Federal welfare expenditures, 1993. Source: *1994 Green Book,* 5, 125, 796.

federal funds. The really big programs are the Social Security Retirement and Disability program, with costs in 1993 of about $419 billion; Medicare, about $143 billion; and Medicaid, $132 billion.[44]

In 1993, the average monthly family enrollment in AFDC was 5 million, of which 359,000 were in the unemployed parent program. This number is an all-time high and is projected to increase steadily, though at a slower pace, to 5.5 million in 1999.[45] The 5 million families translates into 13,626,000 recipients, of which 9,225,000 were children.[46] This represents about 63 percent of the children in poverty.[47] Adjusting for inflation, the average grant per AFDC recipient in 1970 was $676 per month and $373 in 1993—a 45 percent reduction.[48]

The greatest increases in the AFDC population occurred between 1988 and 1992, when the number of recipients grew from 10.9 million to 13.6 million. Although unemployment rates are clearly responsible for a portion of the increase, they are not the only factor. In some states, unemployment rates declined while AFDC rates rose. In spite of the recent increases, AFDC recipient rates for the total population actually declined by 4.8 percent between 1975 and 1992.[49]

Who are the AFDC recipients?

Most (45 percent) mothers have never married; less than a third (30 percent) are divorced or separated.[50]

Between 1969 and 1992, the average AFDC family size *decreased* from 4.0 persons to 2.9. In 72.7 percent of the families, there are one or two children. Another 15.5 percent have three children. And there are four or more children in 10.1 percent of the families. The average AFDC family is either about the same size or slightly smaller than the average non-AFDC family.[51]

Very few AFDC mothers are teenagers. Teen mothers, of course, are of special concern. Of the 7.6 percent of AFDC recipients who are teen mothers, more than half are 19, more than 80 percent are over 18, more than 90 percent are over 17, and less than 2 percent are 15 or younger. In fact, the rate of teen births was much higher in the Eisenhower years than it is today. What has changed is that the teens

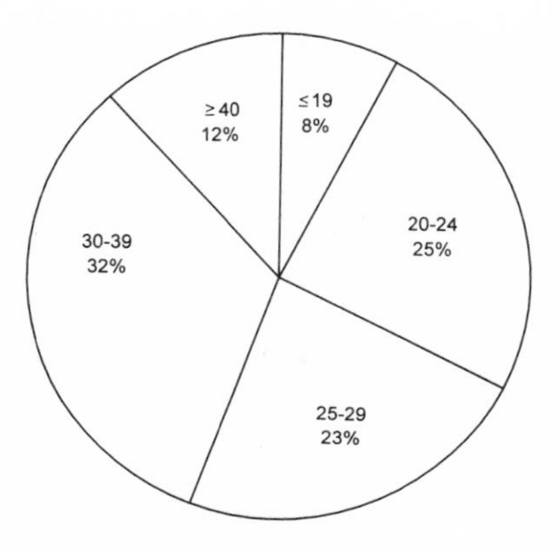

Figure 2 Age of AFDC mothers, 1993. Source: *1994 Green Book,* 401.

are not getting married. Teen pregnancy became a social problem in the 1970s when attention began to be paid to the harmful effects of teen motherhood.[52]

Whites account for 38.9 percent of the AFDC population, African Americans 37.2 percent, and Latinos 17.8 percent.[53]

About half of the children are younger than six; a quarter are younger than three.[54]

At this point, we have established that AFDC parents are mixed racially, are for the most part in their twenties or thirties, and have about two children, about half of them preschoolers. We turn now to education and welfare spells.

About half of the mothers have not graduated from high school. Only about 10 percent have attended post-secondary school. Only about 1 percent have graduated from college. And most score in the bottom quarter on standardized tests of general aptitude and ability.[55]

How long on welfare? The stereotype behind the current debates on welfare reform is that although some recipients are on

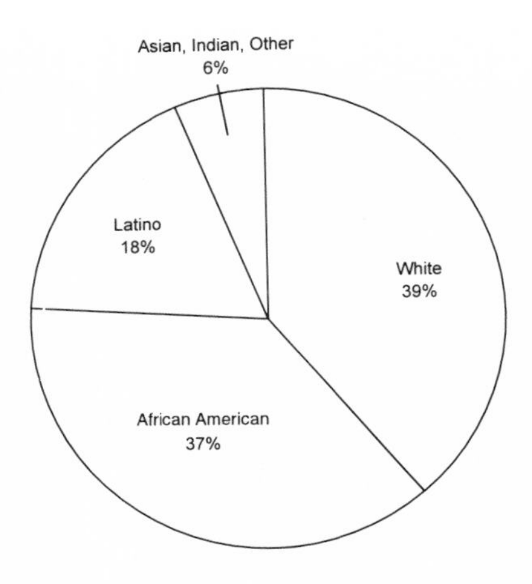

Figure 3 Race of AFDC population, 1993. Source: *1994 Green Book,* 402.

welfare for a short time, for most, welfare becomes a "way of life." This commonly held view is perpetuated in part because most empirical studies of AFDC are based on annual data—that is, they seek to answer the question of whether a particular person was on AFDC at some particular point during the year. Even so, based on annual data, half are on welfare for two years or less and 62 percent are on welfare for four years or less.[56] For whites, 44 percent of welfare spells last only one year and 22.8 percent last an additional year; for blacks, the corresponding numbers are 33.7 percent and 16.2 percent.[57]

Length of time on welfare is only part of the story. Research based on *monthly* data shows a very dynamic welfare population. Not only do people go on and off welfare, but a significant fraction (about one-third) have more than one spell. It is estimated that during the first year of welfare, half the recipients exit AFDC within one year and about three-quarters leave within two years.[58] But many women who leave welfare rapidly also return within the first year. The longer a woman can stay off welfare, the less likely she is to return. Even

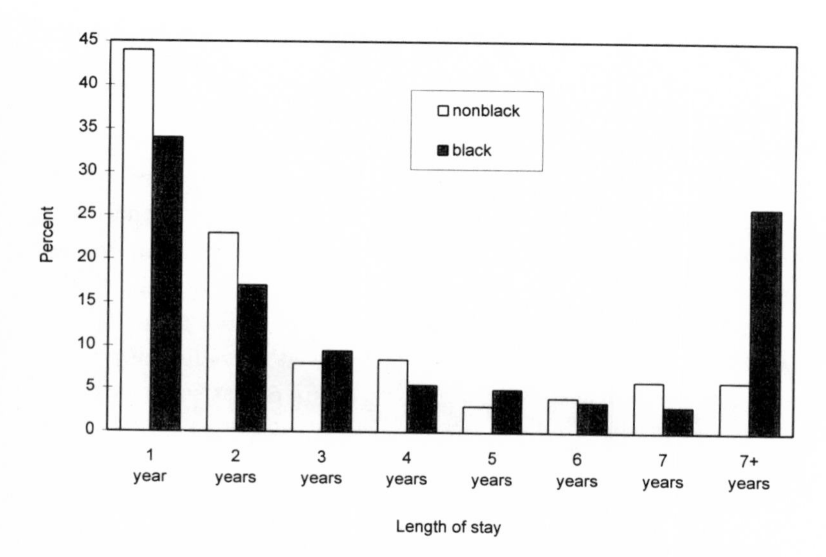

Figure 4 Length of Stay on AFDC, by Race, 1974–1987. Source: Adapted and reprinted with permission from Sheldon Danziger, Gary Sandefur, and Daniel Weinberg, eds., *Confronting Poverty: Prescriptions for Change* (Cambridge, Mass.: Harvard University Press, 1994), 94.

counting multiple spells, 30 percent are on welfare less than 2 years, and 50 percent are on welfare less than 4 years. Only about 15 percent stay on welfare continuously for five years. The overall picture is that one group receives welfare for short periods of time and never return. A middle group cycles on and off, some for short periods and others for longer periods, but again, not for five *continuous* years. And a third, but quite small group stays on welfare for long periods of time.[59]

What, then, accounts for the commonly held view of the long-term welfare recipient? Even though most welfare spells are relatively short, at any one time a majority (65 percent) of persons enrolled are in the midst of what will be long periods of receiving welfare benefits. This is because the probability of being on welfare at any given time is necessarily higher for longer-term recipients than for those who have shorter welfare spells. Thus, even though the typical recipient is a short-term user, the welfare population at any point in time is composed predominantly of long-term recipients. The example that the House of Representatives Ways and Means Committee uses to illustrate this point is as follows: "Consider a 13-bed hospital in which 12 beds are occupied for an entire year by 12 chronically ill patients, while the other bed is used by 52 patients, each of whom stays exactly 1 week. On any given day, a hospital census would find that about 85 percent of the patients (12/13) were in the midst of long spells of hospitalization. Nevertheless, viewed over the course of a year, short-term use clearly dominates: out of 64 patients using hospital services, about 80 percent (52/64) spent only 1 week in the hospital."[60]

The most powerful predictor of long-term welfare receipt is the young, never-married woman. She is usually disadvantaged at least threefold: no high school diploma, no significant employment experience, and a very young child. She is probably also a minority. But even among this group, no more than a third will be on welfare for as long as ten years. As Mary Jo Bane and David Ellwood write, "Long-term welfare is still very much the exception."[61]

Several studies have now documented that the most common route out of AFDC is through work.[62] Many recipients attempt to exit via work but for a variety of reasons—lack of health care, a breakdown in child care, low wages, and jobs that do not last—return to welfare. Still, by the end of six years, more than 40 percent will have left to enter the labor force.[63] Of those who leave welfare through earned income, about 40 percent remained poor after their exit. The picture that emerges from the studies of welfare spells and exits is that for most recipients, welfare is a safety net rather than a "way of life."

Generational welfare is also a myth. A significant majority (80 percent) of daughters who grew up in highly dependent homes (defined as receiving at least 25 percent of average family income as welfare payments) do *not* become dependent themselves. Only 20 percent were themselves highly dependent on AFDC in their early twenties; and 64 percent of daughters with welfare backgrounds received no AFDC.[64] However, there is a higher likelihood that women with welfare backgrounds will receive welfare. The fraction of daughters from highly dependent homes who themselves become highly dependent (20 percent) is much greater than the fraction of daughters from nonwelfare families who become highly dependent (3 percent). And although more than three-fifths of the daughters who grew up in AFDC-dependent homes received no AFDC themselves, more than nine-tenths of those who grew up in nonrecipient families received no AFDC in their early adult years.[65]

There is a relation between intergenerational welfare, but there is no solid evidence that welfare *causes* welfare dependency in the next generation. The powerful effects of poverty and single parenthood probably make it more likely that daughters growing up in these conditions will be poor themselves. As Peter Gottschalk, Sara McLanahan, and Gary Sandefur state:

> Because families receiving welfare are poor—indeed, poverty is a condition of welfare receipt—we would expect children from welfare families to have higher rates of poverty and welfare use as adults than children from nonpoor, nonwelfare families. Intergenerational correlation, therefore, does not necessarily indicate a causal relationship. Daughters and their mothers may simply share characteristics that increase the probability of their both receiving assistance. For example, if both mother and daughter grow up in neighborhoods with poor-quality schools, both will be more likely to have lower earnings and, hence, a greater need for income assistance. . . . Changing the quality of the school the daughter attends . . . will raise her income and, in turn, lower the probability that she receives public assistance.[66]

We have seen that most welfare recipients are neither teenagers nor long-term dependents nor having lots of children. What about dependency, or, more specifically, what about the work ethic of welfare mothers? Is it true that welfare saps the work ethic?

Both qualitative and quantitative data address the work ethic of welfare recipients. A recent study by Kathryn Edin and Christopher Jencks examined empirically the economic position of AFDC recipients in Chicago.[67] They found an extensive amount of work for the simple reason that single mothers on welfare cannot pay their bills on welfare alone; they have to obtain additional income, often without telling the welfare department. The authors based their conclusions on a study of the Illinois welfare system between 1988 and 1990. At that time, a single mother with one child, counting both the welfare grant and food stamps, received $399 per month, or $4,800 per year. Benefits rose per additional child, to $9,300 if she had four, but were still only 60 to 75 percent of the poverty line. Edin interviewed fifty welfare families in Chicago and the suburbs to see how they got along.[68]

Almost all of the recipients obtained additional income, both legal and illegal, to cover their expenses, by work, by receiving money from friends and relatives, or by someone else paying expenses. Recipients had to obtain this income because unless they lived in subsidized housing, the AFDC check would not even cover rent and utilities. For those living in unsubsidized housing, rent and utilities came to $37 more per month than the welfare check; those living in subsidized housing had $197 extra—still not enough to get through the month. Food stamps helped, but again, very few were able to feed their family for the entire month on food stamps alone. Taking the sample as a whole, recipients spent $314 a month for food, rent, and utilities. This left only $10 for everything else—clothing, laundry, cleaning supplies, school supplies, transportation, and so forth. Edin calculated that her sample spent about a third of what the average mother in the Midwest spends on these items. Still, it amounted to $351 in excess of the welfare grant, and almost all of this came from unreported income.

Almost half of the extra money needed to live was earned but not reported. Jobs varied. Some held regular jobs under another name and earned $5 per hour. Others worked off the books (bartending, catering, babysitting, sewing), earning an average of $3 per hour. A small number sold drugs but earned very little ($3–5 per hour). The only high earners ($40 per hour) were occasional prostitutes (in the sample, five).

The families' expenses were about $1,000 per month. The federal poverty line in 1990 was a little less than $10,000. This meant that the recipients consumed $2,000 above the poverty line. As previously discussed, the poverty line is low, and most Americans think it should be considerably higher. Edin estimated that the public would put the figure for her sample at about $16,000, or $4,000 higher than the recipients were presently consuming. Almost all of the sample (88 percent), to varying degrees, lacked basic necessities and material comforts. Edin reported that they lived in bad neighborhoods in rundown apartments, often without heat and hot water. Roofs and windows leaked. The sample had no telephones or money for entertainment. They could not afford fresh fruits or vegetables. There were some small "extravagances," such as renting a video, eating at McDonald's, and purchasing cigarettes and alcohol, but these amounts were just 6 percent of the sample's expenditures. Half of the sample could have cut expenses if they were willing to move into Chicago's worst neighborhoods or the large public housing projects, but they considered these areas too dangerous.

The Chicago results have been replicated in Cambridge, Charleston, and San Antonio. Urban welfare mothers need about $11,000 per year to live on, which they get from work, family, male friends, and absent fathers. Working mothers need even more money to pay for transportation, clothing, and child care. These mothers typically spent between $12,000 and $15,000 per year.[69] Circumstantial evidence, Edin and Jencks argued, suggests that their findings can be generalized. Both rent and living necessities appear to vary little across major metropolitan areas.[70] If these estimates are only reasonably accurate, then in no major American city can welfare recipients get by on their grants. Furthermore, in several states, grants are less than $200 per month for a family of three, and no family can get by on that small sum.

Edin and Jencks compared their results with the Consumer Expenditure Survey for 1984–85. Although that survey is problematic, over 80 percent of the single adult welfare families report outside income. The average is about 40 percent in excess of AFDC and food stamps, consistent with Edin's findings.

If these mothers are so willing to work, why, then, are they also on welfare? According to Edin and Jencks, "Single mothers do not turn to welfare because they are pathologically dependent on handouts or unusually reluctant to work—they do so because they cannot get jobs that pay better than welfare."[71] This conclusion is supported by recent quantitative research that examined the dynamics of work and welfare.[72] As stated, most recipients leave welfare for work. Moreover, a great many (more than half) leave during the first year. The problem is that many also return, and then try again and again. There is significant movement between welfare and work. At least one-half work for at least some of the time that they are on welfare. Although there is some variation depending on the survey, significant numbers —as high as two-thirds—of welfare exits occur when the mother finds a job or continuously works until she leaves welfare.[73] The failure to make a successful exit from welfare is not because of a failure of the work ethic—these women say they prefer to work *and they validate their attitudes by their behavior.* They simply cannot make it in the labor market. Not surprisingly, those who are the most disadvantaged in terms of employability are the least successful. As Gary Burtless puts it, "Even if welfare recipients had no young children to care for—and almost half have children under six—most face severe problems finding and holding good jobs. Limited schooling and poor academic achievement doom most AFDC mothers to low-wage, dead-end jobs."[74] Nevertheless, in spite of these odds, in the words of Kathleen Harris, "Work is much more common in poor single mothers' lives than previously thought, in spite of their very low wages, risk of losing medical care provisions, and child-care constraints."[75]

Contrary to myth, most welfare mothers are adults, they have few children, and they are not long-term welfare recipients. Furthermore, there is no problem about their work ethic. Most either work or try to work while on welfare, and most leave welfare via work. The "problem" of welfare dependency is not the recipients. Rather, the problems are the job market and the conditions of work. In addition to poorly paying, unsteady, increasingly part-time work, are the difficulties of a lack of benefits, especially critical health insurance, and child care.

Nevertheless, welfare policy insists on putting the poor to work by concentrating on the individual rather than on the labor market. In the next chapter, I put together what we know about labor markets and welfare recipients with programs that try to set the poor to work.

4 Setting the Poor to Work

The consensus on welfare reform is that able-bodied welfare recipients should work. Yet, reforming welfare by setting recipients to work seriously mischaracterizes the past and present behavior of welfare mothers, has been tried and found wanting for the past twenty-five years, and shows little promise for the future. Because this policy misconceives both the problem and the solution, it will again lead to collective frustration and repeated victim-blaming of poor, single mothers. In short, it is another exercise in symbolic politics at the expense of the welfare poor.

As we have seen, in spite of the rhetoric of public policy and in spite of the persistent myths of dependency, the vast majority of female heads of households in poverty have *always* had to work. This was true over the long history of welfare, well before the first ADC programs; it was true during the ADC and AFDC periods; and, as recent data show, it remains true today.

Work requirements for welfare recipients were a state and local concern until late 1967, when the federal government enacted the Work Incentive Program (WIN). The year of the program is no accident; by this time ADC recipients had become increasingly black and never-married. And that's when welfare became a "crisis." The initial response of the liberal Kennedy administration was rehabilitation. The administration believed that families would become self-supporting through social services. ADC became Aid to Families with Dependent Children (AFDC), and states were encouraged to provide services to "strengthen family life" and to maximize "self-support and personal independence."[1] Nevertheless, both the rolls and costs kept mounting. In an angry move, Congress abandoned the service strategy in 1967 and again decided to set the welfare poor to work. This was a period not only of increased welfare costs but also of the specter of black single mothers and out-of-wedlock children, urban riots, and increasing racial tensions in large cities. Politicians were responding to the outrage at the local level.

Two strategies can be used to increase the work effort of welfare recipients—regulatory requirements and incentives (the stick and the carrot)—and Congress has regularly employed both. The oldest strategy is the regulatory one. It requires work by either reducing or denying aid and forcing the poor into the low-wage labor market or requiring work as a condition of receiving aid. Symbolically, a regulatory strategy separates the working poor from the welfare poor by stigmatizing welfare recipients. In an earlier age, this work meant confinement and labor in the poorhouse or "pauper labor," such as chopping wood or breaking rocks. Pauper laborers today clean parks and highways, clothed in orange vests, or perform service work under special, differentiated conditions (no benefits, different hours, and so on). The working dependent poor are separate; they are outcasts. The work ethic is affirmed by deterrence and stigmatization.

In contrast, the incentive strategy attempts to encourage recipients to work by reducing the effective marginal tax rate on their earnings or through other forms of employment-related subsidies. By combining work with welfare, recipients will always be better off financially. Symbolically, the incentive strategy blurs the distinction between welfare recipients and the working poor; therefore, it is strongly resisted by those who believe that labor discipline must be enforced through segregation and stigmatization. But the two ideologies have much in common. Both view poverty as a personal deficit rather than as a structural, societal problem.

There is currently a curious paradox in public policy. As I discuss in chapters 6 and 7, there are strong incentives—one in place, the Earned Income Tax Credit (EITC), and one proposed, raising the minimum wage—that will encourage welfare recipients to increase their work efforts. But these programs apply mainly to the working poor and are not considered welfare reform. Instead, the current welfare policy debate focuses on the stick—regulatory work programs for welfare recipients. These programs, both past and present, are the subject of this chapter. The experience of these programs demonstrates that they are largely ineffective in either reducing poverty or substantially reducing welfare rolls. Yet, as a nation, we insist on repeating past failures.

The Work Incentive Programs

The Work Incentive Program combined both incentives and regulatory requirements, but the regulatory strategy predominated. Although recipients were able to keep more of their earnings, the core policy was coercive. Welfare was contingent on participation. Congress expected all adults and children over age sixteen, including mothers, to participate. The penalty was reducing the grant for noncompliance. The legislation contained exemptions—for example, disability or if participation would not be in the best interests of children—but required all "appropriate" persons to register and be referred to state employment services for training and employment services. Day care was promised. Recipients could be excused for "good cause," which was not defined.[2]

Not much happened. Between the time WIN was enacted and fiscal 1971, total AFDC expenditures were more than $4 billion. The additional expenditures for WIN were $150 million. Although more than 2.7 million employment "assessments" were made, just 24 percent were deemed "appropriate for referral" to the employment service, and from this pool, only 118,000 were enrolled in programs. There was further attrition, and, in the end, only 2–3 percent of the eligible recipients obtained jobs through WIN. Moreover, only 20 percent of those who were employed held their jobs for at least three months. At the same time, few recipients were sanctioned. The vast majority of AFDC recipients were excused from participation by officials at the local level.[3]

The program was largely symbolic. It was myth and ceremony. The myth was that recipients were now going to be required to reduce their dependency through training and work. This affirmed the symbol of the work ethic, which was being threatened by rising welfare rolls. The ceremony was requiring able-bodied recipients to register for training and employment.

With these results, the welfare crisis continued to boil. Richard M. Nixon's Family Assistance Plan (FAP), which would have greatly expanded the incentive approach, was defeated by both the right and the left amid fears of further eroding the work ethic, increasing poverty, and blatant racism,[4] and in 1971, Congress enacted WIN II, a tougher program. Mothers with children aged six or older were now required to participate, direct job placement was emphasized over education and training, and sanctions were strengthened. The able-bodied welfare poor were to be forced into low-status work. Mandatory job search became the primary focus—simple to administer, at minimal cost, placing the responsibility on the recipient to find a job.

WIN II failed, too. Its budget grew to more than $300 million and stayed at that level until 1981, when it began to decline. Still, this was wholly inadequate for the more than 1 million recipients now required to register, and they were still only 40 percent of AFDC recipients. Registration turned out to be a "paper" requirement. Only half of the registrants were selected to participate, and the rest were put on "hold." Of those who participated, 25 percent gained employment, but 70 percent of these claimed to have obtained their jobs on their own. Under the best scenario, WIN II removed less than 2 percent of the AFDC recipients from the rolls and reduced grants by an additional 2 percent.

WIN II failed for the same reason as WIN. The funding formula created incentives to cream—that is, put resources in those recipients most employable to begin with. Local offices were faced with the triple problem of uncontrollable local labor markets, multiple employment barriers facing AFDC recipients, and a demand for services that far outstripped resources. No wonder they resorted to creaming and paper registration. Finally, because of lack of resources and the desire on the part of local offices to have good evaluations, sanctions were minimal.[5]

Jimmy Carter and Ronald Reagan

President Jimmy Carter also tried welfare reform—in 1977, he proposed the Program for Better Jobs and Income (PBJI), which was a complex mixture of incentives and regulation. The unique feature of PBJI, which foreshadowed present reform efforts, was a two-tiered welfare system. Recipients considered "able-bodied" (which included mothers with children over six) would receive only half the benefits. They would be required to participate in job search programs, training, and, if necessary, subsidized public employment. This would have been a sharp return to first principles. Under traditional welfare, the able-bodied (undeserving) poor are denied assistance and forced back into the labor market. Because AFDC benefits are considerably below the poverty line, Carter's grants for the able-bodied would have been below subsistence—that is, the old-fashioned way of increasing work incentives. This was why a liberal administration had to have a program of public jobs as a last resort; otherwise, families would have starved. In any event, Carter's proposal failed. Conservatives objected to the creation of public jobs. Liberals insisted that the government should guarantee employment before cutting benefits. Southern states saw threats to their social institutions. Northern states objected to the low level of benefits. And the increased costs were estimated at $14 billion.

As always, race figured prominently in the policy debates. There was little doubt that a major part of the "crisis" of welfare was due to the changed racial composition of the recipients. At the same time, gender issues both changed and remained the same. The big change came with the domestic code. With the dramatic entry of women, including mothers of small children, into the paid labor force, women were now expected to earn income. Poor women, of course, always had to work, but now the rhetorical *justification* had changed, and liberals joined the chorus. The problem is that welfare mothers have an even harder time making successful transitions to the labor market than women in general. They are poorer, have less education, fewer skills, and less work experience, are disproportionately minority, and have more disabilities. The rhetoric of reform now demanded that they enter the paid labor force, but the programs were designed so that only a few would do so. The great bulk would remain on welfare; they would, once again, be considered failures, affirming the value of those who could succeed. By now, the symbols of the mothers' pensions had been turned on their heads. In that day, poor mothers who did not work affirmed the values of the patriarchal domestic code. Now, poor mothers on welfare who could not work would be considered deviants.

This brings us to the Reagan years. As welfare continued on its journey of "crisis," labor discipline, race, and gender discrimination were affirmed and hardened through the continued segregation and stigmatization of the welfare poor. The Reagan administration's principal changes were to restrict eligibility, cut back sharply on incentives (thus redrawing the line between the working poor and the welfare poor), and encourage states to experiment with various work programs by reducing federal WIN funding. Legislation enacted in 1981 eliminated welfare recipients' major income deduction (the first thirty dollars they made and then a third of their further earnings) after four months of benefits.

The Reagan administration was successful. In the 1980s, WIN funding declined, state funding increased, and more than half of the states adopted work requirements—WIN Demonstration Projects.[6] These state demonstration projects provided the background for the Family Support Act of 1988 as well as for Bill Clinton's proposed Work and Responsibility Act of 1994.

State WIN Demonstration Projects

State projects enacted in the 1980s varied.[7] States with relatively strong economies tended to emphasize job placement, training, and support services. Economically depressed states emphasized work-for-relief. Although there was great variation among the states, overall accomplishments were modest. According to a report issued by the General Accounting Office in 1987, about 22 percent of AFDC recipients nationwide participated.[8] As with WIN, however, participation did not necessarily mean receiving services. Approximately 70 percent of participants received services. Of these, 72 percent participated in job-search counseling, 12.5 percent received some form of training, and 11.7 percent received direct placement assistance. The Manpower Development Research Corporation (MDRC), the principal evaluation organization, found that the employability of participants increased by 5–7 percent over control groups but that most jobs were in entry-level, low-wage occupations with a median wage of $4.14 per hour and that almost half of the participants who obtained jobs remained on welfare.[9] The differences in the states varied, not surprisingly, according to differences in local labor market conditions. Areas with strong economies at the time, such as Massachusetts and San Diego, offered work program participants very different opportunities than regions with weak economies.

The San Diego experiment influenced California's GAIN (Greater Avenues for Independence) program, which in turn became a model for the Family Support Act JOBS program. San Diego had two approaches: job search and job search followed by required work.

Under the first, there was a three-week workshop and two weeks of self-directed job search in a group setting. Under the second, if the participant was unable to find a job after job-search, he or she was required to work in an unpaid, public, private, or nonprofit job (Experimental Work Experience Program, or EWEP). The monthly work hours were determined by dividing the family's AFDC grant by the minimum wage. At the time of the experiment, San Diego was experiencing rapid economic growth. Local politics strongly identified with reducing welfare through work. And the education and work history of the participants were higher than the national welfare population average.[10]

Participation levels in the San Diego program were high, although three-quarters of the sample were at some time identified as noncompliant and 10 percent were sanctioned. Yet most participants had positive attitudes toward the program, including the work assignments. Again, although the results were positive, they were modest. For the women (AFDC), employment rates were between 5 and 10 percent higher than those in the control group. Welfare savings were very modest. With the men (AFDC-Unemployed Parent), there was no consistent increase in employment or earnings, but there were significant reductions in welfare payments because grants were reduced as a result of earnings and sanctions. With AFDC, participants gained between $313 and $367 over the course of the year, while the taxpayers lost between $87 (EWEP) and $215 on job search per participant. In AFDC-UP, it was the reverse—recipients lost while taxpayers gained, but again the figures were modest.

San Diego also experimented in a Saturated Work Initiative Model (SWIM), which sought to test the feasibility and effectiveness of including a high proportion of mandatory WIN eligibles in an ongoing job-search, work experience, and education and training program.[11] Although the targeted monthly participation rates were 75 percent, the actual monthly rates averaged 22 percent for program-arranged activities and 33 percent if participant-initiated education and training were included. In view of the characteristics of the families and the administrative burdens, the researchers concluded that the participation rate was probably the best that could be expected. This is an important finding, because there is a public misperception that all welfare recipients of working age not only should but could participate in a work program. Yet a committed, well-functioning agency could not enroll half of its target population. As I discuss later, the current reform proposals require high participation rates and seek to impose penalties on states that fail to meet the targets.

SWIM achieved "significant" gains in employment (12 percent over the control group) and "modest" earnings—$354 per participant the first year and $656 in the second year. There was also a reduction in welfare payments—$407 in the first year and $553 in the second. But although the government saved, the economic well-being of the participants hardly improved. Indeed, AFDC applicants experienced a net loss ranging from $878 to $883, whereas SWIM recipients experienced about the same gain.

In spite of these very modest results, policymakers used the research findings to implement state programs. Two of the leading innovators were Massachusetts and California. Massachusetts's Employment and Training Program (ET) was, for all practical purposes, voluntary, while California's GAIN program continued the carrot-and-stick approach.

Massachusetts's ET Program

When ET started in 1983, Massachusetts was already enjoying the lowest unemployment rate in the country—3.9 percent. In the three preceding years, AFDC rolls had *declined* 29 percent, due in part to a robust economy and in part to the Reagan administration's welfare reforms. The decline in the rolls continued while the state economy remained robust. Under ET, recipients were required to register but not required to participate. Instead, ET provided incentives to participate through an array of services, including education, training, and child care and transitional child care and health care for recipients who left welfare via employment. ET was expensive. State appropriations reached $68 million (1988), averaging approximately $2,000 per participant per year. Participation was high (67 percent of all adults); about 50 percent were active beyond the initial assessment and orientation. Of those who participated, 44 percent obtained jobs with a mean starting wage of $5.70 per hour. Of those who found jobs, about 49 percent stayed off welfare.[12]

There are criticisms of ET. It is claimed that voluntary participation and performance-based contracting resulted in selecting the most employable recipients and that costs rose and participation fell as ET exhausted this pool and began to recruit and train the less employable. Starting wages were higher for participants in areas with tighter labor markets and for participants with the following characteristics: male with previous work experience, short welfare spells, and participation in vocational training. Scholarly opinion is divided on the effects of ET—that is, whether the program or the economic effects reduced the caseload.[13] In any event, the favorable economic conditions were a major influence on the politics of ET. When favorable conditions change, one could expect the program to change, and that is exactly what happened. As the economy of Massachusetts declined in the late 1980s and the budget deficit increased, political support for the expensive ET program disappeared. Welfare rolls increased but funding declined. Massachusetts is now leading the states in tough welfare reforms. The lesson is that as long as times are good and welfare rolls and costs are declining, states will be generous. When times are hard, cheap old-style work requirements return.

The California GAIN Program

GAIN emerged in 1985 as a patchwork of compromises from contending ideological perspectives that were fueled by continuous rises in AFDC rolls and declining public support for tax increases. After much controversy, liberals accepted mandatory work while conservatives agreed to a package of services to help recipients become employable. Like Massachusetts, the basic idea is that all eligible recipients are to participate in programs until they become employed or are off AFDC. Mothers whose children are three years or older are eligible. There are provisions for volunteers. Recipients undergo orientation and appraisal before they are slotted. Those with work experience, for example, go immediately into job search. Others might go to remedial education. Employment plans are developed for those unable to find jobs, and work-for-relief is provided for those who complete the plan but fail to find a job within ninety days. Work-for-relief can last up to a year, and then the process begins again.

The program is full of contradictions. GAIN was expected to deter the able-bodied yet, according to its promises, offers an attractive package of services. It is supposed to give priority to long-term recipients, yet performance-based contracts with vendors encourage creaming. The program emphasizes job search and placement but concedes the need for services for long-term recipients. Although the ultimate aim is to move recipients from welfare to jobs, numerous safeguards enable recipients to refuse jobs that pay less than the monthly AFDC grant. With all the deductions and allowances, a mother with two children could refuse with good cause a job paying $1,100 per month. There are complicated procedural safeguards and numerous permissible excuses for lack of participation (such as emotional and mental problems, substance abuse, and family crisis). The program is to provide extensive services but has a built-in disclaimer in case resources are lacking. Although the program is mandated by the state, implementation is left to county initiative. GAIN is funded from a combination of new federal funds, new state funds, and a redirection of existing state funds appropriated to state agencies that are mandated to serve welfare recipients, such as adult schools, community colleges, and employment programs. The device of reallocating existing state resources—called maintenance of effort—sets up conflicts at the local level for scarce resources.

Almost immediately, in late 1985, GAIN suffered budget reductions because of California's serious financial difficulties, and counties complained of underfunding. Familiar patterns of participation emerged. Only about a third of those who registered actually attended an initial program component (such as basic education or job search); almost two-thirds were deregistered or deferred.[14] Initial assessments revealed that much higher than expected proportions of registrants had basic literacy deficiencies, in effect changing GAIN from a jobs program to a massive compensatory education program.[15] This may have long-term benefits for recipients, but it also prolongs participants' stay in the program, increases the costs, and strengthens the pressure to move registrants into job search rather than remedial education.

Not surprisingly, shortly after GAIN was enacted, Governor George Deukmejian stated that "GAIN should be transformed into a true 'workfare' program, where immediate priority is to remove people from the welfare rolls and put them on payrolls as quickly as possible." Deukmejian especially objected to the extensive emphasis on education. After pointing to some rare misuses of education funds (for example, graduate education), he proposed that participants be required to look for jobs before being diverted into education or training. As he put it, "Let the job marketplace, not caseworkers, determine who is employable."[16]

Finally, because GAIN depends on an extensive network of county services and counties vary in the availability of these services and the willingness and ability of the services to cooperate with welfare departments, there is wide variation in the operation of the program. Los Angeles County, which contains a third of the state's caseload, has experienced severe difficulties in starting up. As a result, in 1990, fewer than 10 percent of the projected eligible GAIN participants were served.

Riverside County

In 1994, the MDRC reported on the benefits and costs of the California GAIN program in six counties after three years of implementation.[17] As the authors state in their report, the Riverside County GAIN program is becoming the standard-bearer or model not only for proposed changes in California but also for the rest of the country. As I discuss in chapter 5, states and, more specifically, counties are becoming increasingly more important in administering welfare. The MDRC report, particularly its analysis and presentation of the Riverside results, is already having a major influence on policy.

Although the MDRC report examined the experience of six

counties, to simplify the analysis here, only three will be compared: Riverside, Alameda (Oakland), and Los Angeles. Riverside is a large county in southern California that combines urban and rural areas. Large proportions of its AFDC caseload lack basic education and are minorities. Led by a charismatic director, Riverside emphasized a strong employment "message," inexpensive job search, and quick entry into the labor market pursuant to the philosophy that a low-paying entry-level job was better than no job at all and could lead to a better job. This message was addressed to the staff as well as to the recipients. The staff was recruited specifically for commitment to the agency's mission and tightly organized. Recipient success was viewed as joint success by the case managers. The staff monitored attendance and recipient job performance closely, provided support services for employment or employment-related problems, and, most significantly, engaged in extensive job development. The county promised employers trained and job-ready applicants "that afternoon." Employers cooperated to save themselves the costs of screening large numbers of job applicants responding to general help-wanted ads.[18] Staff performance was rated, in large part, on job development and placement. The staff was closely supervised.[19]

Alameda County had a much larger proportion of long-term AFDC African American inner-city residents, with high proportions "in need of basic education." Alameda was distinctive in its emphasis on basic education and training to prepare recipients for higher-paying jobs.

Los Angeles County had a third of the state's welfare caseload, as well as a large inner-city, long-term AFDC population, and enrolled only those "in need of basic education." In addition, the Los Angeles welfare population had the highest proportion who were not proficient in English, the highest proportion who were of color, and the lowest proportion with recent work experience. The Los Angeles program had difficulty in getting under way, and its caseload per GAIN case manager was the highest among the counties.

The MDRC study was based on 33,000 recipients, randomly

assigned between an experimental group and a control group, who entered GAIN between 1988 and mid-1990. Although the authors are appropriately cautious, they conclude that GAIN has been successful and, more important, that the Riverside program has been a substantial success. The report states that Riverside had "unusually large . . . earnings gains and welfare savings. . . . These impacts were the biggest for any of the six counties, and are greater than those found in previous large-scale experimental studies of state welfare-to-work programs."[20]

What was Riverside's "substantial success"? The MDRC first compared the earnings of those in the experimental group with those in the control group for each of the three years of the study and then compared the totals. Over the three-year period, the earnings of those in the experimental group increased by an average of $3,113 over the controls, a 49 percent gain. Welfare payments were reduced by $1,983, a 15 percent reduction compared to the control group. These were the biggest impacts—both earnings and welfare savings—of any of the six counties.

The MDRC method of presenting the *three-year totals* for earnings of the participants might make sense if one were considering a long-term growth investment fund, but it makes little sense in considering the material well-being of welfare families living on the edge, as Edin and Jencks have described. For these families, monthly or even weekly differences in income are the important amounts. When we look at the monthly differences, then the Riverside recipients who worked in, say, year three, averaged only $84 more per month in earnings than the controls, or less than $20 more per week.[21] Edin and Jencks, on the basis of sampling hundreds of recipients in several cities, say that the average AFDC family spends about $1,000 a month. Applying this to Riverside would mean a difference increase of about 8.5 percent in earnings of the experimental group as compared to the control group. In addition, participants experienced reductions in welfare grants—not only AFDC but other programs, such as food stamps. When the reductions are calculated, then the difference in well-being between the experimental group and the control group is even smaller. On the basis of the three-year total, the Riverside—again, the "best"—experimental group was $1,900 better off than the control group, or $52 per month on average.

As the report notes, employment offers many other benefits, such as self-esteem, positive role models, independence, and so forth. But there are also costs. Furthermore, the fact that the control subjects earned nearly as much as the experimental subjects indicates that the control subjects were also working, as Edin, Jencks, and other researchers have argued. The closeness in the monthly outcomes between the experimental and control groups confirms Edin and Jencks's findings about recipients working in the informal economy. Riverside may be only getting the experimental subjects to switch to the formal economy. In any event, the benefits to the recipients of the Riverside program—the best of the bunch—are extremely modest.

What about benefits to the public—that is, welfare savings as compared to the costs of GAIN? GAIN is expensive as compared to earlier programs, primarily because of its emphasis on education and training. On average over a five-year period, the county departments and the other nonwelfare agencies spent about $4,415 per recipient. The *net cost* per person in the experimental group varied widely from less than $2,000 in Riverside to more than $5,500 in Alameda and Los Angeles. In Alameda and Los Angeles, more long-term recipients were enrolled in education and training. The report found a positive benefit-cost ratio in Riverside but not in Alameda or Los Angeles. That is, for every dollar invested per person in the experimental group (not counting public education and training that the control subjects received on their own), it got more than a dollar back in the form of reduced AFDC and other benefit programs and increased taxes from increased employment. "This return was exceptionally large in Riverside—$2.84 per every net $1 invested."[22]

In spite of the rhetoric about impressive results from the California GAIN program in general and the Riverside program in particular, small differences run throughout the entire report. For example, the difference in employment between the experimental and control groups was only 6 percent for the entire sample, and in Riverside, it was only 9 percent, and this is for reported employment. But perhaps the most important statistic is that *about two-thirds of the experimentals were not working at the time of the third-year interview, and almost half never worked during the entire three-year period.*

Riverside had a higher earnings impact because the experimental subjects had higher employment rates, but the jobs that they held paid about as much as the jobs of the control group. In Alameda, in contrast, fewer got jobs, but more of the jobs were full-time as compared to the controls, and the wages were higher.

With the small amount of earnings and the nature of employment, most recipients who worked—whether experimentals or controls—also remained on welfare. For the entire sample, only about 19 percent worked and were off welfare during the last quarter of the follow-up as compared to 16 percent of the control group. In Riverside and Alameda, the differences were slightly larger. As to participants' permanently leaving welfare, in Riverside there was a 4 percent point difference (39 percent of experimental subjects versus 35 percent of control subjects).

Regarding specific subgroups of recipients, Riverside showed consistent positive (but "modest") results for those who were found *not* to need basic education and those who were found to need basic education. It is noteworthy that Riverside achieved these gains for those in need of basic education without increasing educational achievement (General Educational Development, GED) or literacy skills among the experimental group. Riverside produced both the "largest" earnings gains and welfare savings among the long-term AFDC recipients (defined as receiving AFDC continuously for at least six years before orientation). The results for the subgroups in the other counties were mixed.

Among all the counties, whites and African Americans experienced the largest gains. The increase for Latinos and for Asians and others was small and not statistically significant.[23] Alameda produced significant and relatively large earnings for African Americans—and its sample was almost entirely long-term and inner-city. Moreover, these gains applied to registrants who were in need of basic education. Three counties had large numbers of Latinos in the sample, but only in Riverside was there a significant earnings gain and welfare reductions for Latinos as well as for whites and African Americans.

Finally, except for Riverside, the earnings effects were "weak" for the most disadvantaged recipients, defined as more than two years on AFDC, no employment in the year preceding GAIN, and a high school dropout.

The MDRC conducted a special study in Riverside to see whether it made any difference if GAIN staff had smaller caseloads. Again, using random assignment, an "enhanced" group (registrant-to-staff ratio of 53 to 1) was compared to a "regular" group (97 to 1). MDRC found no difference in results; thus, at least in running a program like Riverside, there seemed to be no disadvantage in terms of program effectiveness in having caseloads of about 100.

The MDRC calculated program costs per experimental subject for a five-year period. Total GAIN costs comprised the money spent for schooling and other contracted services. Net costs were total public expenditures, including post-GAIN activities minus the public cost of non-GAIN services to control subjects. The average cost for all counties was $2,899 per experimental subject, with Riverside the lowest and Alameda and Los Angeles the highest. Most (60 percent) of the money was spent on case management services (for example, orientations, appraisals and assessment, assignments, and responding to noncompliance). Other expenses included either direct services or contracting (job clubs, supervising job searches), child care, transportation, and equipment. When costs of nonwelfare agencies (education, training) are included, then the average cost per experimental subject was $4,415. Again, Riverside was the lowest, and Alameda and Los Angeles were the highest. The net costs—subtracting the total cost per control subject from the total cost per experimental subject—was $3,422, with the same results in terms of Riverside, Alameda, and Los Angeles.

Turning to cost-benefit findings, the MDRC considered earnings effects not only on AFDC payments but also on Food Stamps, Unemployment Insurance (payments, fringe benefits, taxes), Medicaid (Medi-Cal) payments, administrative costs for AFDC and other transfer programs, and the net cost of employment-related services. The cost-benefit calculation did not include such intangible effects as self-esteem, stress, or loss of time with the family. The analysis also did not include the displacement of other workers, on the grounds that these effects could not be measured.

In five of the six counties, experimental subjects did have a net financial gain; the average was $923 *over the five-year period.* Riverside experimental subjects had the largest gain—$1,900—and Los Angeles experimental subjects experienced a net loss of $1,561. From the perspective of the government budget (reduced payments and administrative costs in transfer programs and increased taxes paid by experimental subjects versus net expenditures for GAIN and non-GAIN services), on average, for the entire sample there was a net loss of $833 per experimental subject, again over the five-year period. The losses were larger in Alameda and Los Angeles counties, reflecting the high education and training costs. Riverside experienced a large net gain—$2,936. Furthermore, Riverside achieved a net gain for recipients who were found to need or not need basic education.

The MDRC concluded from the study that the Riverside results are the "most impressive results ever found for a large-scale welfare-to-work program." The authors also concluded that GAIN could substantially increase the earnings of long-term recipients, although here the results were not consistent across all counties. Different results suggest that different combinations of strategies should be used at the county level. The most important elements should include basic education, vocational training, and postsecondary education; a positive message conveyed to recipients about the benefits of employment; and direct job development. Basic education, which is both the most innovative and the most expensive part of GAIN, has had mixed results. It certainly, in the words of the report, "offers *no guarantee* of success—even when it is extensively used (as in Alameda) or its quality is considered exceptional (as in San Diego)." The fact that in most counties members of the experimental group who lacked basic skills did not achieve significant earnings "suggests that attempting to get as many of these recipients as possible to attend basic education as their initial GAIN activity appears not to be the most productive strategy." Or, that long stays in these activities requires close supervision and perhaps job search "along the way." The lesson MDRC draws is that counties should emphasize job search as well as basic education.

For members of the experimental group who did not need basic education but did use vocational training and postsecondary education, Alameda County participants got better jobs and achieved the greatest overall financial gains. This strategy was costly for the government, however; in fact, there was a negative net investment per experimental subject from the standpoint of the government's budget. Furthermore, in Riverside and San Diego counties, this subgroup also achieved large earnings and substantial welfare savings *without* vocational training and postsecondary education (as compared to the control group). The approaches in Riverside and San Diego may thus be more cost-effective, even though the recipients would not get better jobs.

The MDRC report, in conclusion, emphasized two distinguishing features in Riverside: "the 'message' about employment that staff attempt to convey to registrants while they are in *all* components, and the active use of job development to establish a close link to private-sector employers." The Riverside employment message permeates the program. Specially commissioned music extolling the values of any job is piped into the waiting areas, and the message is even beamed to registrants in education and training. "Perhaps," says the report, "[the message] contributed to Riverside's success by affecting how much effort registrants—across a variety of subgroups—made to look for a job, and how selective they were with regard to the kinds of jobs they would accept."

Job development also applies throughout the Riverside program; that is, all registrants are provided a "direct link" to employers, and this may also increase "*opportunity and incentive* to apply in the labor market what they learn in GAIN activities." No single factor, says the report, can account for Riverside's uniform results across all subgroups; rather, it was the combination of the pervasive employment message, job development efforts, the use of job search among all registrants, a strong commitment to securing the participation of all the mandatory registrants, and a willingness to use sanctions to reinforce the seriousness of the requirements.

The MDRC cautions that it is not clear whether the Riverside program could be replicated elsewhere. The variation among the Riverside offices suggests that it could. Yet the emphasis on job development and quick employment may not work in inner-city areas (Alameda and Los Angeles) or more rural areas with high unemployment. Finally, the report conceded that "GAIN, even operating at its best, was only moderately successful in moving people off welfare and out of poverty by the end of three years."

Beginning in 1987, Florida tried to employ the Riverside approach statewide.[24] Its program, Project Independence, placed its emphasis on up-front job search. The state agency established job placement goals and placement competition among Florida's counties. Use of threats of sanctions was high—24 percent of participants received sanction notices, although only 3 percent were actually sanctioned. Yet no county even approached Riverside's numbers. After one year, 55.3 percent of the experimental group were ever employed during the year, as compared to 52.5 percent of the control group, a difference of 2.8 percent. Average total earnings for the experimental group were $2,540 and for the control group $2,383, or a difference of only $157—for the year. Moreover, the increase in first-year earnings were concentrated among those participants with no preschool children and those defined as job-ready. Of the experimental group, 85.1 percent were on welfare at least some part of the year, as compared to 86.7 percent of the control group. In this state at least, Riverside could not be replicated.

The Family Support Act's JOBS Program

With the exception of Riverside, the GAIN experience seems to differ little from the country as a whole under the Family Support Act. The Family Support Act's work program, JOBS (Jobs Opportunities and Basic Skills Training Program), went into effect in 1990. Because of major problems in reporting the data, it is hard to know what is going on. Not only is there great variation among the states, but there is great ambiguity in the reporting categories. Nevertheless, the evidence so far does not look promising. Overall, about 13 percent of recipients are "assisted by JOBS," but this could range from merely registration to actually participating in a program component. The best estimate is that only about 10 percent of adult AFDC recipients are in a program component, but again, there is great variation. In twenty-four states, less than 10 percent of families are in a JOBS component activity, in forty-one states, less than 20 percent. Yet the states seem to be meeting the congressional targets for the "hardest to serve"—that is, 55 percent of JOBS resources are to be spent on long-term, young mothers who have not completed high school or have no work experience or who are about to lose eligibility owing to the age of their children.[25]

Although one cannot be sure, it seems that the largest percentage (32 percent) of those participating in JOBS are in basic education programs, which is in sharp contrast with WIN. Basic education can include high school/GED completion for adults, school activities for teenagers, and English as a Second Language (ESL) courses. Skills training accounts for 16 percent of JOBS participants. Fifteen percent are in job search; 7 percent are in job readiness activities, which are intended to prepare participants for work through orientations, assessments, and so forth; and less than 1 percent of recipients are in on-the-job training or work supplementation.[26] It appears that although some states are not using workfare, programs in which recipients are required to work a certain number of hours for their grant, other states are relying quite heavily on workfare. Overall, just 3.7 percent of registrants are in workfare programs.[27]

Education and Training

The big difference in the Family Support Act, as compared to prior welfare-work programs, is the shift toward education and training. If one combines education, skills training, postsecondary, and self-initiated components (that is, recipients who are already enrolled in school), then about half of JOBS participants are in human capital development. It is hard to know how this will turn out. Most of the evaluation research studied job search or job search combined with work experience and did not include a substantial education component. Although both Harris and Pavetti found that education, along with mastery of basic skills and work experience, was related to long-term exits from welfare, the most recent study of long-term, basic education for AFDC recipients—the MDRC study of California's GAIN program—is not promising.[28]

The MDRC study examined the effects of basic education and training.[29] The programs studied were classes in Adult Basic Education (ABE), which focuses on reading and mathematics; preparation for the GED test; and ESL. The report emphasized, at the outset, that this was an evaluation of *mandatory* basic education services, and not "adult education services as they are normally delivered: to people who seek them out and participate in them voluntarily."[29] This is an important point. In five of the six counties, the county contracted with existing adult education services, and no special provisions were made for welfare recipients. In the sixth county—San Diego—program administrators recognized that welfare recipients had special needs since this was a group that had had, for the most part, unsatisfactory experiences with the education system, including school failure and dropping out, and therefore might be reluctant to start again. County administrators assumed that existing adult education services would not suit the GAIN population because of these negative experiences. Accordingly, San Diego County established a new countywide program exclusively for GAIN recipients. A network of centers (classrooms) provided a more intensive program that included computer-assisted learning combined with classroom instruction, integrated academic and life skills instruction, off-campus instructional sites, a new teaching staff, and classes for adults with learning disabilities. In addition, special services, such as counseling, attendance monitoring, and support, were provided. San Diego assigned special case managers to spend a significant part of each week at the schools helping the participants, especially in resolving attendance problems. Educational outcomes in San Diego were better than in other counties.

In the six counties, 58 percent of GAIN recipients were found to be in need of basic education and were referred. Of those referred, 71 percent attended programs. Those who were referred but did not attend were either temporarily excused, found jobs, had health problems, or had other legally acceptable excuses. The participants attended classes for about eight months on average but were in class for only about 60 percent of the scheduled time. Even though monitoring procedures were in place, attendance was inconsistent. Of those who participated, only 20 percent had completed basic education within an eleven-month follow-up period, another 20 percent were continuing after the follow-up period, and 60 percent had stopped without finishing. Participants stopped either because they were employed or because of health problems. San Diego, and the one other county, Alameda, that, as noted, put resources into monitoring, had the highest completion rates (almost 40 percent). Those who had higher literacy rates to begin with were more likely to achieve the GED or the high school diploma, and in less time, as compared to the more disadvantaged recipients (those with lower literacy scores and a longer time receiving AFDC). This last finding, concluded the MDRC report, indicates that recipients with lower educational levels will require more education and stay longer on welfare.

As for educational *attainment*—most participants achieved the GED rather than the high school diploma—GAIN was successful in most of the counties, especially for the recipients who were more literate to begin with. Educational *achievement* was measured by the Test of Applied Literary Skills (TALS).[30] Here, only one county, San Diego, saw large and significant improvements. The other counties saw no improvement in basic math and literacy skills. Yet, even in those counties in which improved educational attainment or educational achievement improved, there was no impact on either employment or earnings within the two-year follow-up period. In three counties, for a small group, there were hints of a "possible growth in earnings impacts" in the third year. The MDRC results are consistent with what Pavetti found—namely, that merely enrolling in GED classes was not effective; education has to be more than standard adult classes.[31]

Similar results have been reached with regard to skills training programs—namely, that they do not result in increased earnings for the participants. A major review of outcomes from the Jobs Training Partnership Act (JTPA), which in 1982 replaced the Comprehensive Employment and Training Act (CETA),[32] found no statistically significant differences in outcomes for most groups; in fact, for teen participants (aged sixteen to twenty-one), the program had negative effects. Adult women made modest gains—after a thirty-month follow-up, subjects in the experimental group earned $5,631 on an annualized basis, as compared to $4,896 for those in a control group, or a difference of $735. Women in the control group still had incomes at just 54.5 percent of the poverty line, and there was no reduction in welfare dependency.[33] The reason for these results, argues Gordon Lafer, is that in the nonprofessional part of the labor market, training is relatively less important to wages than other institutional determinants, such as lack of unionization, the minimum wage, the expansion of contingent labor, the lack of enforcement of workplace regulations, discrimination, and the influence of global markets. Contrary to popular belief, data from employers do not indicate any increase in the demand for skilled labor. "In service occupations, which provided the greatest job growth over the decade, only 35.5 percent of workers needed training. . . . Data entry and telephone clerks commonly earn $6 per hour as temp workers with no benefits, sick days, or seniority."[34]

Before the MDRC and JTPA studies were published, most analysts thought that education and skills training would *in the long run* improve a recipient's prospects of economic independence. Now the case has to be made. Meanwhile, the upfront costs are high and the ultimate savings to the taxpayer unclear. In the past, states have either been impatient or unconvinced and, after a relatively brief period, cut back on basic education and training. This is now happening not only in California but in practically all of the proposed welfare reforms. Increased emphasis will be placed on job search programs to move recipients into low-wage, entry-level jobs. Job search is the least expensive component of reform programs and has the potential for the highest short-term payoff for the state even though most recipients will scarcely be better off.

There are no national data on other JOBS outcomes—no information on whether participation has led to changes in employment, in average entry wage rates, in retention rates, in benefits, in gains from education, or even in the effectiveness of the use of sanctions. According to Mark Greenberg, some states are reporting bits of data—for example, average entry wages varied from $4.44 an hour to about $6.75 an hour in 1993, but most states do not report the number of hours worked. Retention rates vary. Because of a lack of uniform reporting requirements, it is difficult to generalize about these programs, but it appears that many participants lose their jobs within a few months and that many of the jobs gained still leave the families in poverty.[35] Nine states reported entry-level wage data for 1993. The range of reported entry-level wages was $4.44 to $6.57 an hour. Assuming a thirty-five-hour week, this translates into monthly wages of $668 to $989. In only one state, therefore, would a family escape poverty ($964 a month).[36]

The Family Support Act requires states to guarantee child care, but again it is impossible to tell how many JOBS participants are in fact receiving child care assistance. If one looks, however, at the total number of AFDC families receiving child care assistance—which is larger than the number of AFDC families in JOBS—then the figure is 3 percent for the nation. The majority of these children are in family day care establishments or center-based care. The median amount of child care expenditures per family per month was $208; the national average is $282. Finally, it appears that most families leaving AFDC because they gain employment are not receiving Transitional Child Care (TCC) assistance. The Congressional Budget Office projected that 280,000 children would be in TCC in 1991, but in fact only 46,000 were enrolled. In sum, although the evidence is fragmentary, it suggests that earnings are low, job loss in initial months is substantial, and transitional child care is underused.[37]

The gap between the rhetoric that accompanies the Family Support Act and the actual performance to date should not surprise us. Given the states' economies and fiscal problems and the level of current funding, it is not reasonable to expect JOBS to do much of anything for the vast majority of welfare recipients. At present, states are spending only about 60 percent of allocated federal funds and serving at most 10 percent of AFDC families. There were 4.4 million adults in AFDC in 1994. Of those, 43 percent, or 1.8 million, were "JOBS mandatories"; just 16 percent of the mandatories were in a JOBS component.[38] In terms of participants, at least as of 1992, JOBS seems to be behind the WIN program. Even if the states spent 100 percent of federal funding, JOBS would probably not reach a quarter of AFDC families—past experience indicates that programs become more expensive per participant the larger the number served. The problem of low participation is not the need for more authority to require participation, it is for more resources to operate programs.

Judith Gueron, president of MDRC and perhaps the most widely quoted spokesperson for welfare-to-work programs, argues that it has been demonstrated that states and counties can implement effective, large-scale work requirement programs that increase employment and reduce welfare receipt.[39] Focusing primarily on Riverside County's experience, she says that the most consistent positive results are from short-term, low-cost job search and work experience (work-for-relief) programs, with varying levels of sanctions. They produce "modest earnings impacts" and "modest welfare savings." However, although "more people got jobs," they did not get "'better' jobs." Although there were "modest increase[s] in total income; many remained in poverty and on welfare," and there were "no consistent earnings impacts among the more disadvantaged." Translated, at best, welfare receipt declined by only 7 percent among the people targeted by the programs, most of those who went to work got relatively low-paying jobs, which triggered reductions in their welfare grants and often substantially offset their earnings gains, resulting in little increase in their combined income from earnings and welfare.[40]

Even though Gueron expresses tempered optimism about the potential for mandated work programs, she points out that unless there is major funding for JOBS, significant welfare reform will not be accomplished. The very limited earnings capacity of most women on welfare—combined with stagnating or falling wages for low-skilled workers—constrains success. Even if they work full time, most women receiving AFDC are not likely to earn much more than they receive on welfare. Single mothers must work full time and have access to jobs paying above-poverty wages, and minimum-wage jobs no longer provide this.

When we put the pieces together—the state of the labor market and the characteristics of the welfare population—we see that single mothers on welfare cannot even approach self-sufficiency through earnings alone. Given their education and skill levels, their labor market consists of low-wage, low-skilled, and most probably part-time jobs with no benefits.

Edin and Jencks calculated the economics for their welfare sample. Single working mothers who resemble welfare recipients in terms of education, experience, and other employment-related characteristics averaged $5.15 per hour (in 1989 dollars). Without a high school diploma, the average wage was $4.10 per hour; even with a high school diploma and 10 years' experience, the average wage was $6.55 per hour. Working full-time (the average is 35 hours per week) for 52 weeks at $5.15 per hour yields $9,360, or less than 80 percent of what Edin and Jencks's welfare recipients presently consume on an austere budget. And, of course, single mothers cannot be expected to work full-time, every week, if for no other reason than that jobs, at this level, are frequently unstable and there are often child care problems. The official unemployment rates among single mothers averaged 10 percent. Thus, if welfare mothers held these jobs, they would earn an average of $8,500 per year, or 70 percent of their consumption needs.[41]

How much would Edin and Jencks's recipients have to earn to be better off than on welfare? At the time of the study, the recipients consumed about $12,000 per year. It costs money to work. If they worked in legitimate jobs, Edin and Jencks estimated the added expenses as follows: $800 for medical care, $300 for clothing, $500 for transportation, and $1,200 for child care. Adding in taxes makes a total of about $16,000, which, they point out, is what most Americans think the poverty line ought to be. With an average work week of about 35 hours and an unemployment rate of about 10 percent, to earn $16,000 a worker would have to receive an hourly wage of $10, which is about the average wage. To earn $16,000, at an hourly wage of $6, they would have to work more than fifty hours per week every week of the year.

What is more likely is that these single mothers would work at $5 per hour, 35 hours per week, for an average of 47 weeks, earning only $8,225 before taxes. They would still be in poverty. They would still be short $7,000 for a very modest standard of living. The federal minimum wage is just $4.25 per hour. As Edin and Jencks point out, the math is simple. The single mother can't make it either by work or by welfare.[42]

Pavetti's study confirms these results. As stated, she found that many recipients repeatedly try to exit welfare by employment but that the economics simply do not work out. Given the low-wage jobs, the lack of benefits, and the costs and difficulties of child care, a great many women are forced to return to welfare. Welfare recipients frequently got jobs as waitresses, bartenders, caterers, cab dispatchers, babysitters—for about $5 per hour with no benefits—but felt that they would have to get jobs, with benefits, that paid about $8 or $9 per hour. Child care—both quality and cost—and health care were major obstacles.[43]

It is easy to see now why past and present welfare-to-work

programs sort out the way they have. In spite of the much-touted success of GAIN and JOBS, the fact remains that few participants are better off economically. This is true in Riverside as well as in other "successful" welfare-to-work programs. The vast majority of welfare recipients are lacking both education and skills, and, as noted, in Alameda, which stressed education and training, GAIN registrants did obtain better jobs at higher wages. Yet *overall* results in Alameda were not as positive as Riverside because many more Riverside registrants were employed; thus, even though wages were lower, program totals were higher. Furthermore, Riverside had a positive cost-benefit ratio and Alameda had a negative one—that is, even though the Alameda registrants were better off individually, it cost the public more. The lessons policymakers are extracting from the MDRC studies are that job search programs with an emphasis on quick employment, even in entry-level jobs, is the way to go.

Clearly, given the chance, lower-level officials will favor education and training. Employment, even workfare, is costly. Welfare mothers are not easy to place in jobs. They have child care problems and health problems. Absenteeism, inevitable with mothers of young children, is not a good way to remain employed. Community colleges and vocational schools may not be tailored to the special needs of recipients, but absenteeism is clearly not as disruptive there as it is in employment. Education satisfies at least some of the reformist and public agenda, and life is easier for the local welfare offices. But education and training are costly and problematic. In California, the Alameda results have been ignored and history is being repeated.

Riverside is the future. The California Department of Public Social Services GAIN Advisory Council, reflecting the MDRC research on Riverside, is recommending that GAIN be refocused on finding immediate work for recipients and on reducing costs. Counties are to be given even more authority in administering the more controversial provisions.[44] Among the recommendations are giving the counties discretion to remove deferrals for registrants who are already working between fifteen and twenty-nine hours per week (this is not considered "self-sufficient"); to include mothers four months after the birth of a child conceived while on welfare; to require drug abusers to participate in a substance abuse program; to substitute county target groups for statewide targets; to allow counties to expand postemployment services; to allow counties more flexibility if they enter into a performance agreement with the state; and to establish county job placement expectations that would be negotiated with the state. Other recommendations would apply statewide: shorten and streamline the conciliation process—for example, allow only one conciliation period before administering sanctions for failure to cooperate without good cause; prevent other aid programs (such as food stamps and rent subsidies) to increase as a result of a sanctioned decrease in the AFDC grant; and require job search as the first GAIN component to "increase the work focus of the GAIN program."[45] The council also favors establishing job-search requirements for all AFDC applicants independent of GAIN (with exceptions for disabilities, child-only cases, and so on).

Mandatory Work Requirements

A final issue is mandatoriness, and here again is another paradox. The evidence over time is both consistent and persuasive that the vast majority of welfare recipients do not lack a work ethic. Empirical work demonstrates, as we have seen, that, against considerable odds, the majority of welfare recipients work while they are on welfare, trying over and over to find and keep jobs, and that, in fact, the majority do leave welfare through work. Udesky reports that when job training and other employment services were offered in the South in the 1980s, tens of thousands volunteered, replicating Leonard Goodwin's findings of more than a decade ago.[46] Kathleen Harris puts the matter bluntly: "Parents rely on welfare simply because they cannot find jobs that pay enough to support their families."[47]

Yet, in spite of the evidence that not only do most welfare recipients prefer to work and try to work—it's not just a matter of subjective feelings—*and* that work and training programs invariably are repeatedly oversubscribed, policymakers insist that work programs be mandatory. Somehow it is incumbent on politicians to "send a message." Lawrence Mead has long argued that welfare programs have to be made "authoritative," that welfare recipients have to be told that they have "responsibilities" along with entitlement, that this is part of the social contract.[48] It is also argued that if most recipients are willing to participate, then mandatory sanctions will be relatively minor. Yet, manditoriness has heavy costs and is counterproductive.

Return to the data on the employment behavior of recipients. It stands to reason that those who do try to leave welfare through work but fail and stay on welfare for longer periods have greater difficulties in entering the labor force. Harris reports that the least successful, or more dependent, have less human capital and have larger families and/or younger children.[49] These recipients also might have more health problems or psychological problems. Whatever the reason, this minority of recipients is less susceptible to such cheap quick-fixes as three-week job search or community-service work relief programs. Sanctions in the form of grant reductions or even termination only increase the hardship. Sanctions do not change behavior—that is, increase the work effort of these recipients. As I demonstrate in the next chapter, the same conclusions apply with requiring teens to attend school: support programs change behavior, sanctions do not. Unless we are interested only in punishment, what recipients need is sustained, long-term investments in their future.

But what about deterrence? Will sanctions have a deterrent effect on those who are on the fence? This is nothing more than the age-old tactic of using "hostages": in the nineteenth century, the poor relief system made life miserable for those who *had* to go to the poorhouse in order to deter the able-bodied poor from taking advantage of relief. Those who are sanctioned can't work but will be punished anyway as a deterrent. This is not only cruel but unnecessary in view of the strong evidence of recipients' work ethic.

Why can't an agency do it all? Provide short-term placement services for those ready, willing, and able to enter the labor market, long-term more professional services for those who have more difficult problems, and sanctions for those who are either on the fence or refuse to cooperate? After all, there is anecdotal evidence from recipients who say, "If they didn't make me come I probably wouldn't have come, but I'm glad I did." Perhaps in an ideal world, one could find such an agency, but in a recent study of four preselected California GAIN programs, Yeheskel Hasenfeld and Dale Weaver found that the approaches are organizationally, if not fundamentally, inconsistent. In counties where sanctions were taken seriously, programs were bureaucratic and rule-oriented, recipients were processed with minimal contact between worker and client, and rates of conflict, noncompliance (absenteeism and so on), and sanctions were higher. In counties that downplayed sanctions (administrators had to mention them because GAIN is mandatory) and emphasized professional, cooperative, supportive, holistic relationships, participation rates were higher and sanctions were almost nonexistent.[50]

Riverside County fits this pattern. Staff members do tell researchers that sanctions are necessary to underscore the seriousness of the work obligation, but in practice, the staff emphasizes positive, supporting, optimistic relationships and goals with the recipients; sanctions are mentioned but distinctly downplayed—they are considered a failure of *both* the agency and the recipient. The supportive attitude is backed up with services for recipients who get jobs but then encounter problems. Well-focused agencies, whether in Riverside or Alameda, do not need sanctions. Sanctions become a counterproductive substitute for the hard work of job development and client-supportive services.

Why, then, do we insist on sanctions when they are at best ineffective and, more likely, counterproductive? We cannot abide those few who refuse to play by the rules. Sanctions, even if fruitless, symbolically affirm that we are in control.

These, then, are the contradictions of very longstanding welfare-to-work programs. Recipients want to work, but even minimally adequate jobs aren't there. Politicians won't fund the costs of what at least a minority of recipients really need. Sanctions are costly and ineffective. Yet the pressure is to reduce welfare costs through mandatory work programs. Work programs, however, even community-service jobs for the welfare grant, will not reduce costs in the short run, and the short run is, unfortunately, the time-frame for policymakers. The only certain way to cut welfare costs is to cut grants. Sanctions do save money; as will be discussed in the next chapter, this, too, imposes costs on local government. What can be done? The inevitable solution, both in the past and today, is to deflect the bulk of the recipients somehow. They can be "referred"; they can be "registered." This satisfies the ceremony of the work requirements, while quietly putting the recipients on hold. Sociologists have a name for this practice—when the political policy demands conflict too much with reality, the program is "decoupled" at the field level—that is, practice is quietly separated from political symbolic demands. This tactic works for a while—as long as welfare rolls and costs remain a dead issue. When rolls and costs become unacceptable, when political demands mount, Americans try again with the same old programs of setting the poor to work.

It is clear that requiring welfare recipients to work for their relief does little to improve their economic well-being. It is also clear that for the majority of women on AFDC, even when they do work, periodic dependency on welfare benefits is unavoidable. The dominant cultural norm of viewing welfare as antithesis to work thus contradicts the social reality, in which work and welfare must complement each other. As long as this dependence is not recognized, work programs will continue to serve their symbolic function while being largely marginal to the social reality of poverty and welfare. At the same time, society collectively will believe that it is "ending welfare as we know it." But if history is any guide, life will go on as usual for the overwhelming majority of welfare mothers. Without adequately paying jobs, they will continue to be blamed for their dependency.

"Unlike the problems of children in much of the world: age-old problems of disease, new problems of ecological disaster, the problems of children in the United States are overwhelmingly associated with the strength and stability of their families. Our problems do not reside in nature, nor yet are they fundamentally economic. Our problems derive from behavior." **Senator Patrick Moynihan**

5 The Return to the States: Changing Social Behavior

The same myths and ceremonies that accompany work requirements also take place with reforms that seek to change social behavior. These reforms reflect a consensus that poverty is primarily behavioral rather than economic or environmental, the fault of the individual. The two most popular of the current reforms are Learnfare, in which benefits are reduced if a child fails to attend school, misses too many school days, or fails to maintain certain grades, and measures designed to discourage giving birth to welfare children. These include the family cap, in which additional benefits are not granted for children conceived while the mother is on welfare, and ineligibility for children whose paternity has not been established or who are born out of wedlock to a mother under the age of eighteen unless the mother marries the father or someone adopts the child. Other proposals require teen parents to live with their parents, provide incentives to marry or to use the birth control drug Norplant, and impose sanctions for rent delinquency and for failure to obtain medical treatment for children.[1]

Many of these reforms are being instituted at the state level. Although under the federal grant-in-aid law, states retain a great deal of discretion over AFDC, states generally cannot impose additional eligibility requirements—such as denying aid for a child conceived while the mother was on welfare—or withhold money for behavioral matters—such as failure to attend school. The Department of Health and Human Services (HHS) has been granting the states waivers to institute these policies. This waiver practice has been going on since 1962, but it became increasingly popular during the Reagan and Bush administrations and increased during the first two years of the Clinton administration. Now, even more state control over AFDC under block grants, with or without federal restrictions, is a central feature of the debate over welfare reform in the new Republican-controlled Congress.

Since 1992, forty states have requested waivers, and twenty-five of those applications have been granted. Thirty-four applications have been filed since 1993.[2] The accelerating pace of the waiver practice represents a significant change in AFDC and deserves scrutiny. In this chapter, I discuss the significance of the waivers from a political perspective before turning to the substance of the more popular waivers—what they purport to accomplish, and what has been the practice. Then, in chapter 6, I examine the provisions of the Republicans' proposed Personal Responsibility Act for changing social values and increasing state authority.

The Delegation Solution

As discussed in chapter 2, the various programs that constitute the American social welfare state are distributed among different levels of government. Programs for the aged—the deserving poor—are administered at the national level: Social Security retirement, survivors, and disability, Supplemental Security Income, and Medicare. Programs for the most undeserving poor—childless, working-age adults—known as General Relief (GR), are handled at local levels, generally the counties (in some states, GR is administered at the state level; in other states, at the municipal level). Programs that are morally ambiguous, where recipients may or may not be excused from work—AFDC, Unemployment Insurance, workers' compensation—are organized at the state level. Although poverty allegedly resulting from the lack of a work ethic is a major moral concern, the undeserving poor invariably bear other negative burdens—race, gender, and ethnic discrimination, fears of vice, deviance, and crime, and the reproduction of generations of dependents and criminals. The undeserving poor, in the past and today, threaten not only labor markets and family values but the social order.

The jurisdictional distribution of welfare programs follows the moral characterization of the class of beneficiaries. This has been the historic pattern. The more ambiguous or more deviant the perceived moral character of the poor, the more local the control of relief. In the nineteenth century, certain categories of the poor were institutionalized—the blind, the mute and deaf, the insane, those orphaned by the Civil War—but this was not for custodial efficiency. Rather, these unfortunates were to be extracted from local relief so that they would not bear the stigma of pauperism. In the twentieth century, the dependent aged were morally problematic. The Social Security Act of 1935 sought to maintain the distinction between aged people who had been steady, reliable workers and contributed from those who were merely poor. The act excluded marginal workers, domestics, and agricultural workers (thus, Southern blacks). The steady, reliable, contributing workers were included in the retirement program, and the marginal workers, domestics, and agricultural laborers were relegated to state old-age assistance and local relief. Gradually the politics of the elderly forced more and more of the dependent aged onto Social Security, but not until the early 1960s were most elderly people allowed in. Then, in 1972, the remaining dependent aged were folded into a national program, Supplemental Security Income; now, all of the aged poor are deserving.

In contrast, the able-bodied unemployed are morally problematic. Why is the person unemployed? Did he or she voluntarily quit or leave work as the result of a labor dispute? Is he or she trying hard enough to find another job? In chapter 2, it was noted that the most important issue during the debates on the Social Security Act was the jurisdictional location of Unemployment Insurance. One would have thought that the unemployed, particularly in such numbers, would be a national problem—as other Western industrialized nations perceive and assist the unemployed. But not in the United States. Local business and Southern agricultural interests wanted to retain control over their labor markets and race relations. Today UI is still administered locally.

In spite of the apparent success of the early ADC legislation, relief for single mothers and their children has always been highly controversial. At issue were such societal values as the patriarchal family, the domestic code, and the perceived responsibility of men to support their families. There were always work requirements, even for the white widows who did receive aid. There were moral requirements, too. The home had to be "fit and proper." The states decided who would receive assistance, how much assistance they would receive, and under what conditions they would receive it.

When ADC became a grant-in-aid program under the Social Security Act, few eligibility conditions were imposed; states still decided financial eligibility, how much relief to provide, who was fit and proper, and who had to work. As stated, until the late 1950s and early 1960s, states excluded most single mothers and their children. During the Civil Rights era and years of the Warren Court, some AFDC eligibility requirements became federalized. States could no longer deviate from eligibility provisions contained in the Social Security Act. For example, "man-in-the-house" rules—in which families would lose eligibility or have their budgets reduced if the mother was found to have had sexual relations with an unrelated male or gave birth to a child conceived while on welfare—were declared in conflict with the Social Security Act.

The increasing federalization of this period, however, though important, should not be exaggerated. For example, the federal work programs, first WIN and now JOBS, have delegated most responsibility to the states. Under the Family Support Act's JOBS program, the states are the key administrators of the work programs. Furthermore, as research conducted by the Manpower Development Research Corporation shows, it is not only the states but the counties who are the most important actors in AFDC programs. And states still retain control over financial eligibility and the level of aid they provide; nothing in the present law or in the various reform proposals takes away the state's authority to set benefit levels and thereby include or exclude large numbers of poor, single mothers and their children. In Alaska and California, the monthly AFDC grant for a mother and two children is $923 and $607, respectively; in Mississippi and Texas, it is $120 and $184.[3]

And yet, what is new is that waivers granted to states now are giving them increasing control over eligibility requirements. In short, there is a significant return of state authority over social and moral behavior to the days before the Warren Court. And, as my discussion of the Republican and Democratic legislative proposals will show, the process of decentralization seems to be moving into high gear.

However the current round of the welfare reform battle is resolved, there is considerable truth to the statement that even now there is no longer a national AFDC program. One could even argue—I certainly would—that there are not even fifty state programs. There are more than three thousand county governments. Perhaps not all run welfare programs. Yet in large urban counties there are multiple offices, each with field-level workers exercising discretion. In many states, AFDC is state-run, but here, I would argue, there is also considerable autonomy in local offices. The general point stands: for a great many crucial AFDC matters, there are hundreds, if not thousands, of local programs.

Although there are probably many reasons for existing patterns of federalism, I think that three are particularly important in understanding welfare. First, welfare, as I have emphasized, often involves deeply felt moral issues, and these moral issues are most keenly felt at the local level. Labor markets, race, sexual relations, child-rearing practices, deviancy, and crime have historically been matters of local control. Citizens in the community do not trust higher-level politicians to be sufficiently sensitive to their interests. Local people insist on regulating the local moral climate.

The second reason is a corollary. The regulation of moral behavior often involves conflict, including assessing taxes and spending public funds, and upper-level politicians, if they can help it, generally seek to avoid such conflict. From time to time, local conflicts over moral behavior erupt and partisans demand upper-level interventions. When demands are made at the upper level, the favored technique is to pass a symbolic gesture and redelegate the conflict to the local level. A successful delegation is one that stays delegated. The initial ADC statutes are an excellent example of the use of delegation to manage conflict. They were born in sharp controversy. The language of the statutes was quite broad (for example, they potentially included divorced, separated, and, in some states, never-married mothers), but discretion was delegated to the local courts, who in turn handed administration over to local charitable organization societies to resolve the conflicts on a low-visibility individual basis. The reformers were satisfied—they established "mothers' pensions"; at the same time, local administration ensured that traditional notions of patriarchy and the domestic code were not disturbed.[4]

The technique of passing a statute but delegating discretion to lower units allows for the third reason: symbolic politics. The early ADC programs were an exercise in myth and ceremony. The myth was that now the state was going to help poor single mothers stay at home and take care of their children. The ceremony was that a few are helped (which supporters could point to); the reality is that life went on as before. And taxes were controlled.

Thus far, federal work programs have been an exercise in symbolic politics. Every time one is passed, it is hailed as a "new" reform that is going to set the poor to work. Instead, as we have seen, few recipients are enrolled and very few get jobs. Discretion is delegated to local offices that have to deal with hard-to-employ recipients but lack any control over local labor markets. In addition, serious work programs require significant up-front costs. The result, as we have seen, is that life changes very little.

Today, there is growing anger about "welfare" and intense focus on "doing something about welfare" by changing the moral behavior of the recipients. This accounts for the substantive provisions of the reform proposals, and especially the negative, sanctioning ones—no aid for welfare newborns, requiring teens to live with their parents, requiring the use of contraception, mandating school attendance, and requiring work. In addition, given budgetary constraints, there is a growing fondness for no-cost solutions to social problems—in this case, by withholding welfare benefits. This is perfect for state and local politicians. They save money (sanctions) and uphold virtue. It's a win-win situation. It seems that almost daily additional states are requesting waivers or getting waivers. Not untypically, William Schaefer, the governor of Maryland, requested waivers to limit welfare to eighteen months to recipients who could not find work or would not accept full-time community service jobs, plus a family cap. The request was newsworthy only because it was endorsed by the Maryland chapter of the National Association for the Advancement of Colored Persons (NAACP).

If enacted at the national level, many of these provisions that seek to regulate moral behavior through sanctions would provoke controversy (this was probably truer during the 1970s and 1980s). Hence, the importance of the waiver policy. In 1962, Congress gave the secretary of Health, Education, and Welfare (HEW, now HHS) authority to grant states waivers from federal AFDC requirements to conduct "experimental, pilot, or demonstration project[s]" that would promote the objectives of the program. The original purpose of the waiver provision seemed to be to improve services. When the bill was being considered, there were no suggestions that states would be allowed to reduce benefits by changing eligibility requirements or that projects would be long-term, statewide, or duplicative.[5]

During the first ten years, waivers were narrowly focused and designed to improve services—child care development projects, integrating various social service programs, caseworker training. This overall trend continued, but in the early 1970s, HEW began to grant a small number of waivers permitting benefit sanctions—for example, mandatory employment. Again, however, these waivers were narrow and of limited duration.

The federal waiver policy changed with the Reagan administration. At first, the administration granted large numbers of waivers for the welfare-to-work demonstration projects discussed in chapter 4. Then, as part of the administration's philosophy of increasing state authority over AFDC—the administration had unsuccessfully tried to convert AFDC into a wholly state-run, state-financed program through block grants—the waiver process was simplified. A Low Income Opportunity Advisory Board was created in 1987 to expedite state requests. The only significant requirement was that the waiver proposals be cost-neutral (that is, not cost the federal government any money).[6] Though little noticed, the board was hailed as "one of the most important gains for federalism in recent years" by the Heritage Foundation.[7]

One of the first waivers granted by the new board, which set the tone for future policy, was Wisconsin's Learnfare proposal. Learnfare imposed sanctions on teenage recipients who failed to attend high school. The Wisconsin waiver signaled the new direction—this was the first time a waiver had been granted to allow a reduction in AFDC payments for deviant behavior that was not a work requirement.

The Bush administration continued the waiver policy. In his State of the Union Address of January 1992, President George Bush said that he would make the waiver process easier for state programs designed to require recipients "to seek work, education or job training," "to hold their families together and refrain from having children out of wedlock," and "to obey the law."[8] By the end of the Bush administration, waivers had been approved or extended in eleven states. The new Democratic administration under Bill Clinton continued the waiver policy—"we need to encourage experimentation in the states," President Clinton told the National Governors Association in February 1993. Clinton kept his word. Shortly after he took office, he approved an eleven-year Wisconsin "experiment" that has the most severe sanctions to date—Wisconsin's welfare-to-work project. Under this program, Wisconsin is allowed to cut off AFDC benefits to recipients after two years—period—whether or not the recipient has found a job. There are no provisions for public jobs. During the first two years, the family is required to work off the benefits. A mother of two children is required to work about forty hours a week in a community work program or spend the same amount of time in a training program. After two years, she is allowed Food Stamps, medical assistance, and, in some instances, housing assistance. It is unclear whether there are any exemptions even for good-faith efforts to find jobs. The Wisconsin plan applies in two counties.[9]

Until recently, the Wisconsin waiver set the standard for severity; HHS is now hard pressed to deny state waivers that fall within the Wisconsin parameters.[10] State waiver proposals have flooded in, and many of them have been granted. More than thirty states are estimated to have asked for waivers that would cover about a third of the welfare population.[11]

Looking at the array of waivers already granted, it seems apparent that just about any change in AFDC will be considered "welfare reform" and justified as an "experiment." The waivers do not even purport to meet standard social science criteria—for example, they may cover an entire state AFDC population, may fail to test alternative hypotheses, and may repeat projects carried out elsewhere.[12] Waivers have even been granted for projects that test hypotheses that have been disproved. There are no provisions for assessing the impact of the projects on the recipients; instead, the emphasis is on changing behavior and reducing costs. Many of the waivers (at least fourteen states) are not objectionable, allowing recipients to keep more earned income without losing benefits; but in many other states, sanctions are to be imposed unless behavior changes.[13] In effect, under the waiver policy, states have been given essentially unrestricted discretion.[14] At the extreme, Tommy Thompson, the governor of Wisconsin, announced in 1993 that Wisconsin would seek permission to withdraw altogether from AFDC and run its own welfare program.[15]

Nevertheless, in spite of the apparent ease of the waiver process, it, too, has taken on symbolic importance. Governors complain that they have to go to HHS on bended knee. It is the spirit of the new Republican Congress and the Contract with America that Washington should get off the backs of the states. Accordingly, the Republicans are proposing that AFDC be folded into block grants to the states and that the states should have a free hand in providing aid to their poor, but that federal expenditures should be capped and AFDC should no longer be an entitlement. The current battle is over what restrictions, if any, to place on the states (discussed in chapter 6).

In addition to work requirements (usually time-limited welfare), as stated, the waivers fall into the following categories: school attendance or grade requirements (Learnfare); family caps (denying benefits for children conceived while their mothers are on welfare); family planning mandates (use of Norplant); immunization requirements; migration restrictions (reducing or eliminating benefits for "newcomers"); and across-the-board cuts. The likely impact of the waivers varies according to the specific state plans. Wisconsin's family cap, for example, is offset considerably by a rise in food stamps.

One of the most significant waivers is the California Welfare Demonstration Project.[16] The state's motive is clearly to reduce welfare costs. In fiscal 1993, California was facing a budget deficit of $6–$10 billion. The state government estimated that the waiver proposal would save approximately $600 million. The plan was initially submitted to the voters, but they rejected it. Then, Governor Pete Wilson submitted the plan to HHS, and the waiver was granted. The waiver allows for two across-the-board benefit reductions—an immediate 10 percent reduction and an additional 15 percent cut six months later.

There are work incentives, a family cap, and restrictions on benefits for "newcomers." Under the California plan, with the work incentives, families would be better off financially if the mother worked at least twenty hours per week at $5.50 per hour, but the reductions apply to all families whether there are earnings or not.

A public interest law firm challenged the California waiver in 1994 on the grounds that, among other things, a statewide cut could not be considered a "demonstration" project and that the state had failed to consider the harm to disabled adults and children-only AFDC families. A lower court refused to grant a preliminary injunction, but this was reversed on appeal to the Ninth Circuit, which remanded the case because the record did not show that HHS had considered plaintiffs' objections to the waiver request.[17] The Clinton administration is not appealing the decision, and it is doubtful whether this decision will put a dent in the waiver practice.[18] Indeed, three days after the decision, Governor Wilson trimmed the waiver request slightly, and HHS is reported to have responded favorably.[19] The matter remains in litigation.

As mentioned, two of the more popular waiver proposals are Learnfare and the family cap. The effects of these two "experiments" are considered next.

Learnfare

Learnfare began in Wisconsin in 1987 at newly elected conservative Governor Tommy Thompson's request. Since then several other states have started similar programs, and a number of states have initiated teen-parent programs under JOBS. The Wisconsin program applies statewide to all teens on AFDC, whether they are parents or not. A teen who misses ten unexcused full days of school per semester is monitored monthly thereafter and is sanctioned if he or she misses two unexcused full days of school in any month. The sanction is the loss of the teen's share of the AFDC grant for that month. For a family of three, in 1991 dollars, this would amount to $77 of the monthly grant of $517. The program is enforced. During the two school years of 1988–90, an average of 2,125 students were sanctioned per month. In 1989, total AFDC reductions were $3,080,000.[20]

The goals of Learnfare are to affirm the norm of mutual responsibility and to increase high school graduation rates. It is true that although high school dropout rates for AFDC mothers are declining, they remain high, and efforts should be made be made to increase graduation rates. However, among AFDC teens in Wisconsin, 92 percent are meeting school attendance requirements. And there is no evidence that AFDC children miss significantly more school days than other children. According to Lucy Williams, "AFDC children, on average, attended school 169 days per year while non-AFDC children attended for 172. Moreover, this data has been consistent over many years."[21]

Teens fail to attend school for a number of reasons that are not subject either to economic incentives (an additional $75 to the mother) or to parental authority. An assistant principal in Milwaukee stated that sanctioned students "are not going to realize the value of an education by docking their parents. We've had youngsters brought here by their Learnfare parents at eight o'clock, and at nine o'clock they're gone. It's in one door and out the other."[22] In fact, the dramatic use of sanctions questions the ability of Learnfare to deter absences.

A study of the effectiveness of Wisconsin Learnfare showed no positive results on school attendance and recommended social services instead. For example, 41 percent of the children sanctioned in Milwaukee were in families that have possible or documented problems of abuse or neglect or were involved with the children's court; less than a third returned to school on a regular basis after being sanctioned. In addition, teenagers may be unable or unwilling to attend school because of violence, inadequate school services (such as alternative education and drug counseling), or because they are needed at home. Learnfare makes the heroic assumption that teens will respond to economic sanctions imposed on the family, that they care enough about the family, or that they will not be tempted to impose a penalty on the family. In short, Learnfare may increase family conflict.

Nevertheless, Learnfare blames the parent. School officials agree—sanctioned students do not return to school, Learnfare has not reduced dropouts. Finally, there are significant problems of errors in reporting absences. The governor fired the evaluation firm. Meanwhile, the number of sanctions has not declined.[23]

In spite of the evidence, however, Learnfare along the Wisconsin model remains popular among many states. From a political point of view, it is a perfect program. It affirms the symbolic values of responsibility and education, it blames the welfare mother, and it saves the taxpayers money. Never mind that it does not deal with the causes of school failure.

Other states, however, are emphasizing services and incentives along with sanctions. The most sophisticated effort to encourage AFDC teens to obtain a high school diploma or a GED is Ohio's Learning, Earning, and Parenting Program for Teenage Parents on Welfare, or LEAP. Three-year results for Cleveland were reported in a MDRC study published in 1994.[24] The Ohio program, begun in 1989, focuses on teen welfare mothers, who have high dropout rates and are most likely to become long-term welfare recipients. All pregnant and custodial parents under twenty years of age who receive AFDC either as the parent or from someone else (usually their mother) are subject to LEAP. They are required to enroll and regularly attend high school or a GED program.

Unlike Wisconsin's Learnfare, LEAP has combined financial incentives with sanctions. If a teen parent complies, she receives an enrollment bonus at the time of enrollment and for each subsequent academic year and an attendance bonus for meeting each month's requirement (two or fewer unexcused absences or four or fewer total absences). Sanctions apply to those who, without good cause, fail to attend assessment meetings, to enroll (or for dropping out), or maintain attendance.[25] In all three years of the study, each bonus and sanction was $62. The combination of bonuses and sanctions could significantly affect a teen's income. For example, the AFDC grant for a teen on her own with one child would be $274. A bonus would increase the grant to $336 and a sanction would reduce it to $212. There would thus be a $124 per month difference between a teen mother in school and one who, without good cause, is not.

For all teen AFDC mothers, LEAP also provided case management, transportation, and child care assistance. In addition, there was a Cleveland Student Parent Demonstration project that offered "enhanced services" beyond LEAP. Enhanced services were of two kinds: school-based, including case managers in schools, in-school child care, and instruction in parenting skills, and community-based (for those teens who were not enrolled), including outreach, special GED preparation classes, and parenting and life skills instruction.

In Cleveland, the direct costs for LEAP were about $971, in 1993 dollars, for the entire period of program eligibility per teen; case management cost $651 per teen (including transportation); child care cost $358 per participant. Sanctions exceeded bonuses, so there was no net cost for the incentive structure; in fact, expenditures were reduced by $38 per teen.

The study found that virtually all teens were affected by the bonus and sanction system. With a typical group of one hundred LEAP teens, seventy-eight earned one or more bonuses, while fifty-two received a grant reduction at the same time. However, although most teens cooperated at least at some point, the amount of sanctioning indicates that cooperation was uneven—of the typical one hundred, sixty-eight received at least one sanction request, sixteen received only sanctions and no bonuses, and ten received nine or more sanctions.[26] On average, teens earned more bonuses early in the program and more sanctions later. Moreover, as the program progressed, the proportion of sanctions increased. Of the 68.2 percent of teens who qualified for sanctions, they averaged 9.2 sanction requests during their time on LEAP, and 45 percent of these teens qualified for nine or more sanctions. LEAP had the least successful results with teens who were not enrolled in school—the difference in the teens who were in school and those who had dropped out was clear. Dropouts accounted for most of the sanctions and for far fewer bonuses. Significantly, 22 percent of dropouts were subjected to repeated grant reductions. As the authors wrote, "This high level of sanctioning implies that many teens are not responding to LEAP's inducements to change their behavior; at the same time, the program is substantially reducing the welfare of some affected families. Moreover, the 'ever-sanctioned' rate of 68.2 percent far exceeds the rates measured in evaluations of mandatory welfare-to-work programs for adults."[27]

The LEAP requirements were minimal for the Cleveland program. The attendance requirement was satisfied by twenty days at school per academic year. School progress was satisfied if the teen passed at least one one-credit course per semester. Completion was the high school diploma or GED. At the end of third year of LEAP, 11.6 percent of the program teens had attended high school in the past year as compared to 9.6 percent of a control group; 6.9 percent of the program teens earned credit as compared to 5.4 percent of control subjects; 14 percent of the program teens completed high school as compared to 11.2 percent of the control group; and 7.1 percent completed the GED as compared to 4.3 percent of the control subjects. Although several of these differences may be statistically significant, "More striking than the impact figures is the fact that so few of the teens in the Cleveland sample completed their schooling."[28]

Under the regular LEAP program, although financial assistance is available for transportation and child care, the teens themselves are responsible for making the arrangements. Under Cleveland's enhanced services demonstration, those in school received in-school child care, case management, and instruction in life skills and parenting practices. Some mothers preferred to arrange child care with relatives or friends rather than participate in in-school child care. Parenting and life skills instructors, as well as case managers, provided a variety of services, including information and counseling, monitoring attendance and progress, providing feedback, removing barriers, solving problems, and conducting home visits. Teens in focus groups spoke warmly of their school-based caseworkers.

For those out of school, there was outreach and special and

enriched GED programs operated by community-based organizations. Outreach proved to be difficult. Workers reported spending considerable time simply trying to locate the teen mothers. Overall, almost a third of those referred for contact were not reached. Those who did not attend gave various reasons—child care, transportation, health problems, wanting to stay home with their children, but according to the MDRC report, the outreach workers were "convinced that often, despite teens' stated reasons for their absences, the bottom line was that they did not truly want to go to school."[29] Those who did attend were often interrupted by family and personal crises. The specially designed GED classes were designed to reach those teens who had had bad experiences with school. In addition to basic education, there were programs on life management, employability development, family planning, health, and parenting.

Costs per student for enhanced services rose from $971 to $2,900 per eligible teen. In spite of the enhanced services, the increased benefits were minor and statistically insignificant. There was some improvement for students already in school; there was no success in encouraging dropouts either to return to high school or to earn a GED. The combined effects of both LEAP and enhanced services helped somewhat.

Consistent with its evaluation of the adult welfare-to-work programs, the MDRC report made the most out of very modest results. The authors claim that LEAP "succeeded in significantly increasing the proportion of teen parents on welfare who earned a high school diploma or received a GED after three years of follow-up." Translated, this means that after three years, 15.5 percent of teen mothers "on their own" received the diploma or the GED, whereas with LEAP, the proportion was increased to 21.1 percent. But even with LEAP, about 80 percent of the teen mothers were still not completing high school or earning a GED. The findings for teens who were not enrolled in school were particularly discouraging. Noted the authors, "The results from Cleveland, though promising, indicate that the combination of incentives and services accomplished less than had been hoped."[30]

In reporting on the effects of welfare-to-work programs, Judith Gueron, president of MDRC, always reminds her audience that these programs can do only so much; by themselves, they do not increase the supply of decent jobs. The same is true with LEAP. As the study noted, "While the LEAP results are positive, there are also clear limits to the program's likely ultimate impact on school dropout rates and long-term welfare receipt. Welfare departments have little control over what teens experience once they are in school. . . . [A] troublingly large number of teens described their schools as dangerous and frightening places where learning was difficult. Clearly, dramatic improvements will require efforts to transform the school environment."[31]

Ohio's LEAP program is ambitious. Its emphasis on incentives and services is commendable, especially in comparison to the usual state waiver demonstration projects. Yet it is flawed because it remains within the old welfare reform model. It focuses exclusively on the individual—in this case, the student—rather than on the environment. Financial incentives, case work, transportation, and child care can help, but they cannot substitute for serious family and social problems or the massive deficiencies of inner-city schools. Still LEAP relies on sanctions even though sanctions are ineffective. As the authors of the MDRC report admit, significant numbers of families are under repeated sanctions, suffering significant losses of income with no change in behavior. Once again, those who have the most serious problems are held hostage to the symbolic needs of a majoritarian society.

The Family Cap

Family cap programs attempt to influence the AFDC mother's decisions about procreation. The first program was enacted in New Jersey in 1992. The program assumes that because middle-class families plan their children on what they can afford, welfare mothers should do the same. The unspoken assumption is that welfare families are large and that it is necessary to curb the practice of welfare mothers having more children to obtain more benefits.

Why family size is an issue is even more puzzling than school attendance. It is true that the proportion of children living with one parent has been increasing, and this is especially true for unwed mothers. For example, in 1980, fewer than 2 out of 10 births were to unmarried mothers; by 1991, 3 out of 10 children were born to single mothers, an increase from 0.7 million to 1.2 million children.[32] This is a serious problem, but it is not one that can be solved by reforming welfare. As we have seen, the size of the AFDC family has been declining steadily for the past several decades and is now roughly the same, if not smaller, than the nonwelfare family—approximately 1.9 children. Almost 90 percent of AFDC families have three or fewer children.

There are many reasons why women—poor women, AFDC mothers, all women—will choose to have children; the argument that welfare is the cause is not convincing. As Sara McLanahan and Gary Sandefur point out in their recent book, recent trends in welfare benefits and single motherhood diverge.[33] Both rose during the 1960s and 1970s, but for the past two decades, welfare benefits have declined while single motherhood has continued to rise. Neither family size nor teen birth rates are higher in high benefit states. In addition, single motherhood is increasing among women who are neither on welfare nor likely to be motivated by the promise of welfare. Finally, in other industrialized countries, benefits for single mothers are considerably more generous than in the United States; yet these countries have lower rates of single motherhood. Empirical evidence shows in fact that AFDC mothers are *less* likely than non-AFDC mothers to have multiple pregnancies and *more* likely to use contraception.[34] McLanahan and Sandefur think that the rise in single-mother families is due to a combination of the growing economic independence of women, the decline in men's earnings relative to women's, changing social norms with regard to divorce, the acceptability of single motherhood, reduced trust in the institution of marriage, and the experience of single-parent families when these women were growing up.

Nevertheless, the family cap is popular.[35] Some mothers will give birth to children while on welfare; some sanctions will be imposed; there will be some cost savings; and there will be an increase in poverty for these families.

Massachusetts

I close this chapter with a discussion of the latest state to have proposed welfare reform—Massachusetts. Previously the home of the Employment and Training Program (ET), the most liberal and by some accounts one of the more successful programs in moving welfare recipients into the paid labor force, Massachusetts has leapfrogged past Wisconsin by enacting the most far-reaching, most comprehensive, and most restrictive of all state programs. Several states may have one or two provisions for welfare reform, but Massachusetts is attempting to do it all. The work requirements include the following: benefits will be cut 2.75 percent for 48,000 able-bodied recipients (although they will be able to retain more money from earnings); those who are able-bodied and have no child under age six (about 18,400 recipients) must get a job or perform twenty hours of community work (workfare) per week within sixty days of going on welfare; paid work or workfare recipients will have to work twenty-five hours per week plus conduct fifteen hours per week of job search; drug or alcohol dependency is not considered a disability; recipients with children under age six must enroll in education or training until their youngest child reaches age six, when they must get a job; and (with some exceptions) no able-bodied recipient will receive welfare benefits for more than twenty-four months in any sixty-month period regardless of whether they have found a job.[36] Employers are to be encouraged to hire welfare recipients by using some welfare benefits as reimbursement for wages.

Rules geared toward changing behavior include: teen-age mothers must live either with their families or in state-run homes and make satisfactory progress in school; no aid will be given to children born to mothers already on welfare; and mothers must identify the fathers of their children, must get their children immunized, and must ensure that their children attend school.

It is estimated that the new program will increase state costs by $17 million, most for day care. The name of the Department of Welfare is to be changed to the Department of Transitional Assistance. Under present law, Massachusetts will need waivers to implement its program, but that should not prove to be an obstacle either on the basis of past waiver policies or, more likely, given the climate of reform in the new Congress. Massachusetts has anticipated Washington's mood.

The state waivers flesh out the remaining elements of the stereotype—in addition to dependency, AFDC families engage in multiple irresponsible behaviors: they have children to get more welfare, they fail to take care of their children's needs, the children do not go school, and they, in turn, become welfare dependent when they get older. And all of this costs the taxpayers more money.

With the notable exception of Ohio's LEAP program, there is not even the pretense that waivers are being granted only to valid demonstration projects. The waivers are, rather, responses to state and local political demands to "do something" about the "welfare mess." From the perspective of state and national politicians, the waivers are a perfect solution. Washington can satisfy national and local demands to respond to the welfare crisis; and national politicians can satisfy state politicians by responding to their political needs. Political controversies over the undeserving poor are delegated back to the local level. The waivers themselves are classic myth and ceremony. The myth is that deviant behavior is now going to be controlled. The ceremony is that there will be sanctions. There will be adults who do not report for work. There will be teens who will not go to school; there will be children who do not get immunized; there will be children conceived while their mothers are on welfare. Yet, by and large, the sanctions are not draconian. Grants are reduced, families will suffer, but probably neither the family cap nor Learnfare, by themselves, will dramatically increase family break-ups and thus increase state and local costs. In other words, the states really are having their cake and eating it, too. They can engage in the myth of welfare reform, not only at little cost, but show welfare savings to boot. In the next chapter, we shall see whether the current reform proposals continue or upset this cozy arrangement.

6 The Current Reform Proposals

As of spring 1995, welfare reform legislation remained unresolved. Contesting the issue are not only the Democrats and the new Republican Congress but the states. And, of course, within these groups there are serious divisions.

The "new" Democratic position, getting tough on welfare, started with Bill Clinton's presidential campaign pledge of October 23, 1991: "In a Clinton Administration, we're going to put an end to welfare as we know it. . . . We'll give them all the help they need for up to two years. But after that, if they're able to work, they'll have to take a job in the private sector, or start earning their way through community service."[1] This was the start of time-limited welfare, one of the three pillars of current welfare reform. Since then, reform proposals from the Republicans and the states have been a series of right-flanking moves—toughening time-limited welfare and adding the two other pillars—family values and state authority.

After much internal debate, the Clinton administration submitted the Work and Responsibility Act of 1994 (WRA). Although the WRA is a very complex bill that covers many subjects, its central feature is time-limited welfare. Meanwhile, the Republicans in the House of Representatives introduced their version of welfare reform, the Personal Responsibility Act (PRA), which later appeared in the Republicans' Contract for America and was reintroduced in the new Congress (H.R. 4). The PRA is really tough: time-limits are tightened; provisions for education and training are sharply reduced; no additional funds are provided for child care; all of the provisions designed to change social behavior (for example, no benefits to children born on welfare or to teen mothers) are included; legal immigrants are disqualified for many aid programs; and by providing funds in the form of block grants to the states, welfare will cease to be a federal entitlement. Although support for the PRA in the House appears to be strong, there is dissent. Important Republican senators have demurred to some of the more draconian provisions, such as denying aid to children because of the sins of the parents, and several Republican governors fear that the PRA will impose additional burdens on states and local governments. And while Washington is debating, as we have seen, welfare reform continues to be good politics at the state level.

In spite of the rhetoric of "real welfare reform," the most likely outcome of this round of legislation is one of great variation in AFDC throughout the country. It is extremely unlikely that there will be a single federal AFDC statute governing the nation; as I have said, that is not true even today. The safest predictions I can make are that state authority will be significantly increased but federal restrictions will remain and that the states will vary on practically all dimensions of welfare reform. I say this because in spite of the apparent unanimity among House Republicans, there really are sharp divisions within the Congress, the administration, the states, and the public over many of the reform proposals.

Given the present state of flux, I have organized this chapter in terms of the major subdivisions of welfare reform: time-limits and work requirements; changing social behavior; and ending the entitlement of status of welfare through block grants to states. I conclude with brief comments about denying aid to noncitizens.

Because concepts of welfare still linger in the shadows of the past, roughly the same outcomes as were seen in the past can be expected from the current round of proposals. Most of the so-called reforms will be on the symbolic level. The hot issues will be delegated to the states—hence, the current popularity of increasing state authority—and the states will try to delegate the issues to the county or local levels. But at the state level, there are counter pressures against the more draconian measures. AFDC, after all, deals with children. Republicans in Congress can protest that they are not starving babies, but they have no control over what happens in the inner cities and the media attention that it receives. In addition to charitable impulses, which may be muted but are never silent, there is the matter of cost. Mothers and children do show up in shelters, and foster care and institutions are far more expensive than welfare. State and local politicians know this. Similar economics apply to other reform proposals. Recall that Massachusetts is willing today to increase the AFDC budget by $17 million in the hopes of achieving future savings, but these savings are problematic at best, and besides, they will be incurred only in the long run. In the end, mandating work requirements is more expensive than providing low-visibility, low-level AFDC benefits. The most likely outcome will once again be myth and ceremony. The myth is that now welfare will really be reformed—it will no longer be a "way of life." There will be some cut-offs, some sanctions, and some success stories. This will be the ceremony. But, for the vast majority of poor mothers and their families, life will go on much as before, unless dramatic changes take place in America's labor markets and the larger environment.

Some new proposals, however, could change the prediction in either direction. Some proposals at the federal level would change the cost equations at the state level, which would increase incentives to sanction welfare recipients. Or, it could be that the nation really is taking a hard right turn. On the other side, there are some important provisions, not considered a part of welfare reform, that could make a difference, perhaps even a substantial improvement, in the lives of a great many poor, single mothers. One measure has long been part of the political landscape but has been dramatically improved under the Clinton administration—the Earned Income Tax Credit. The other is the increase in the minimum wage proposed in January 1995. Important parts of this equation—health care reform and child care—remain to be addressed. These provisions, I believe, would greatly improve the ability of single mothers to engage successfully in paid labor and would reduce welfare dependency. They are rarely, if ever, discussed in terms of welfare reform, a matter I take up in chapter 7.

The heart of current welfare reform proposals—to "end welfare as a way of life"—are time-limits and work requirements, to which we now turn.

Time-Limited Welfare and Work Requirements

Time-limited welfare traces its origins to liberals; it is usually attributed to David Ellwood, currently assistant secretary of HHS, but a professor at Harvard University's John F. Kennedy School of Government at the time he formulated the idea. In 1992, Bruce Reed an aide to presidential contender Bill Clinton picked up the idea, seeing an opportunity to change AFDC from "permanent welfare" to "transitional aid." It was Reed who wrote the campaign speech in which candidate Clinton pledged to "end welfare as we know it."

The seeds of ending welfare "as we know it" fell on fertile ground. The concept reflects the stated aims of the "new" Democrats as well as the liberals who have joined the "consensus" on contemporary welfare reform. The most complete statement of this approach is found in *Mandate for Change*, issued by the Progressive Policy Institute.[2] A much shorter statement is found in Bill Clinton and Al Gore's book, *Putting People First.*[3] *Mandate for Change* contains a familiar discussion of how welfare is undermining the American values of "work, family, individual responsibility, and self-sufficiency" and discusses various state experiments, including, among other things, Learnfare, the family cap, increased efforts to obtain child support, and incentives to encourage earnings and marriage.

A key concept in both books is the subsidization of low-wage work. This idea, first developed by Ellwood, is to make work pay, principally through the expansion of the EITC, the provision of child care and health benefits, and improved child support enforcement. The goal is to make sure that people who work full-time—who "play by the rules"—are still not in poverty (see chapter 7).[4] But the big idea is to set the recipients to work by limiting welfare payments to two years. As we have seen, time-limited welfare is prominent in state waivers as well. In spite of the Clinton package's several important provisions addressing low-wage work, poverty, and child support, unfortunately, but not surprisingly, it is the two-year limit plus mandated work that is receiving all the attention.[5]

It is hard to see how time-limited welfare makes any sense. The two-year time frame, as we have seen, is based on a misconception of the welfare experience. It assumes that most families become dependent on and continue to receive welfare for long periods, whereas the opposite is the case.[6] Almost three-fourths of families beginning a spell of AFDC can be expected to exit before reaching the two-year point. Moreover, there is a great deal of movement on and off welfare even within that two-year period. Many who leave welfare also return.

The actual, as contrasted with the assumed, experience of welfare recipients seriously compromises programs for basic education and training. As noted, the reason for the apparent lack of success of basic education and training for welfare recipients has been that many of the programs fail to take account of welfare population dynamics. These programs are designed for students whose eligibility is not based on welfare rather than for people who are more likely to go on welfare not when the classes start, who are in and out of welfare, and who now face a two-year limit. To reduce costs, WRA has a phase-in (PI) provision for mandatory registration. The requirements start with those recipients most likely to be long-term—young, with young children, less education, and less work experience—but this group is also more likely to have had bad school experiences and to need more intensive services. Yet even this group is actually in and out of welfare. What if recipients are not able to complete a two-year education and training plan? If they exit welfare before the two years are up, they may either not start the program or leave before they complete it—which completely defeats the purpose. And what if they return? Do they start over or continue with what remains of their time?

The fact that many poor, single mothers are in and out of AFDC in a relatively short time raises the question of whether a two-year requirement of education and training is even appropriate—at least at that particular time in these women's lives. The crisis may be only temporary; given time, they may be able to reestablish themselves. In the meantime, the two-year clock is ticking.

There are other problems with the two-year rule. Programs that have available placements would be favored even though they are not necessarily appropriate, because delays would mean that valuable education and training time would be lost. Would administrative delays in starting a program be calculated against the recipient? What about delays caused by illness or lack of child care? What would be good-cause extensions? The welfare cut-off is not just less education and training but a welfare termination after two years.[7] WRA tries to resolve some of these problems with very complicated provisions for starting and stopping the welfare clock.[8] In sum, those who are in favor of providing welfare recipients with basic education and training have made their own case much more problematic by embracing the two-year limit.

Yet, the issue of how to provide basic education and training may very well be moot. *Mandate for Change*, for example, firmly rejects expanded education and training on the grounds that they are "extravagant," not cost effective, and not proven to work. Instead, the argument goes, the two-year welfare period should be spent in low-budget job-search efforts. WRA reflects the New Democrat credo: the

JOBS program will be refocused from education and training to job search and quick employment. JOBS employability plans are "to lay out the fastest and most effective way to help the participant find employment and become self-sufficient."[9] The PRA and the state requirements follow the same path—in short, the Riverside model.

As we saw in chapter 4, the results of Riverside County's GAIN program are not promising, despite all the rhetoric. Even assuming—and this is a large assumption—that the Riverside program can be successfully replicated elsewhere, let alone throughout the nation—most welfare recipients in that program were not working at the end of not two but three years, most of those who were working were also receiving welfare, and almost all were still in poverty. This raises an obvious question: What will happen at the end of two years? This question, of course, applies to all time-limited proposals—those put forth by the congressional Republicans and the states. The Democrats provide for subsidized work or workfare. The Republicans and the states provide nothing—welfare will be terminated.

The Democratic proposal—called WORK—is that if the recipient can't get off of welfare via a private sector job, they will be required to take a community service job. In the states, the model most often discussed is work-for-relief ("workfare"), in which the grant divided by the minimum wage equals the required hours. How many people would be sent to work-for-relief? Mark Greenberg calculates the numbers as follows: At any one point in time, close to half the recipients have been on AFDC for at least two consecutive years, which would be between 2.5 and 3 million families. Not all would be required to participate, but if even we assume generous exemptions, this still leaves between 1 and 1.5 million people. This is a lot of placements. In the entire JOBS program, which involves half a million families, fewer than 30,000 were in a workfare activity. How much would this cost? Figures cited in a recent *New York Times* article estimate that the required number of jobs that would have to be created ranged from a "low" of 500,000 to 1–2.3 million jobs. A work program that enrolled 2.3 million would cost about $14.5 billion a year; with expanded training, the bill could be as high as $20 billion. Even the low estimate of 500,000 would create a work program of unprecedented size: figures for the "scaled down" version are $7 billion.[10] It is hard to imagine that American taxpayers will be willing to spend this kind of additional money to give welfare recipients jobs.

Workfare jobs are problematic. They are costly in that work-related expenses, administration, and child care have to be paid in addition to welfare—the Congressional Budget Office estimates are $6,300 per recipient *in addition to the welfare grant*[11]—and they displace regular employees. There are other costs with workfare. Los Angeles County, for example, runs a workfare program for single men receiving General Relief. In spite of fairly aggressive marketing, the county cannot persuade other government agencies or nonprofits to take free labor for even the most menial jobs. Only 40 percent of recipients are placed. It's not that the men are ne'er-do-wells; rather, employers are reluctant to use welfare recipients, there is union opposition, there are administrative costs, and there is competition for jobs. In other words, workfare recipients are not "free labor."[12] In the targeted wage subsidy experiment conducted in Dayton, Ohio, to give another example, job seekers who were given vouchers identifying them as eligible for wage subsidies were significantly less likely to be employed than those without vouchers. Researchers speculated that the voucher holders were stigmatized and served as a screening device for employers who discriminated against low-income ("welfare"?) job seekers.[13] For a variety of reasons, private employers think that it is cheaper (counting bureaucratic costs) and more efficient to hire "nonwelfare" labor. And when all is said and done, what results from these efforts? Thus far, the evaluation literature contains no findings that workfare increases employment rates or earnings.[14]

As noted, we now have solid evidence that many welfare recipients are working or have had recent work experience. Nevertheless, the WRA workfare proposal would apply to a person who has completed two years of training but has not yet found a job or someone who was on welfare for two years, worked for a year, and was laid off and is back on welfare. That person would be placed immediately in workfare. In short, a large sum of money is to be committed to a program that shows no evidence of increasing employability and would in many cases be counterproductive.[15]

What kinds of jobs would workfare recipients get? There is a serious problem of equity here. If workfare jobs are calculated on the minimum wage but would also have benefits, then how could they be reserved for welfare recipients when so many other Americans are unemployed or underemployed in part-time jobs that lack benefits? Conversely, if workfare jobs do not have these benefits, then it is unfair to the welfare recipients who have "played by the rules." They have completed their education and training, they have tried to find a job, and now they have to perform a subminimum work-for-relief job.

Then there is the issue of job requirements. If a regular employee is fired or otherwise "not retained," that person is eligible for unemployment compensation or AFDC. What happens with a workfare recipient who doesn't or can't perform or has personal problems? If the workfare system is supposed to simulate "real" employment, then sanctions could be very severe—there would be no safety net for the mother and the children. The workfare participant would have exhausted her welfare grant. She might not qualify for unemployment compensation; and if she did, benefits are low and limited in duration.[16]

For those who have reached the twenty-four-month limit and have not found an unsubsidized job, under WRA the states would have to create WORK positions. These WORK positions could not last more than a year. The WRA WORK placements differ from workfare in that the registrants would be paid wages. WORK placements would resemble regular employment in terms of wages and benefits—and WORK participants would qualify for Medicaid regardless of whether they continued to receive AFDC—but in other respects, WORK placements would differ from regular employment. If the WORK registrant worked the full number of required weekly hours (between fifteen and thirty-five), then the family could not receive less income than if it were receiving AFDC with no other income; the family would receive an "earnings supplement," rather than welfare. Although this situation would only apply in high-benefit states, it is not "ending welfare as we know it," and conservatives have spotted this inconsistency.

What if the WORK participant or her children were sick? She would receive sick leave pay from the employer only if the employer provided similar benefits to similarly situated employees. If the employer did not provide those benefits and if she had to take time off because of illness, however, there would be no AFDC adjustment to make up for the reduced earnings. Thus, if a mother had to stay at home because a sick child could not go to school or to day care, the family would lose a day's pay.

Most significantly, WORK income would *not* qualify for the Earned Income Tax Credit, and WORK participants would *not* be covered by Unemployment Insurance. The theory for denying EITC coverage is that recipients would then have an incentive to seek unsubsidized employment. Again, the rationale is historic welfare policy: the principle of "less eligibility"—benefits would have to be lower than those of the lowest nonwelfare workers.

WORK assignments could vary from fifteen hours per week to thirty-five, on average, at the state's discretion. If the WORK assignment was for fewer than thirty-five hours per week, the state could require the participant to engage in additional job search. (Under the Republicans' PRA, there would be no discretion—recipients would have to work a thirty-five-hour week.) As stated, WORK assignments could not last more than twelve months, and an individual could not be reassigned to the same position. If the participant was still unable to find an unsubsidized job, then the state could defer the person, assign the person to JOBS, to another WORK assignment, or to an intensive job search program.

Under the WRA, the age limit for young children would be

down to age one; the vast majority of states exempt parents of children under age three. For a child conceived while the mother was on welfare, however, the mother will be deferred for just twelve weeks. Present law prevents a mother of a preschooler from being required to accept a job that requires more than twenty hours per week; this protection is removed. Other restrictions would tighten existing rules—for example, requiring written confirmation from a licensed physician for an excuse of illness or incapacity, removing automatic exemptions for recipients under sixteen who are full-time students, and so forth. There would penalties for failure to sign an employability plan; there would be a new penalty for failing to participate in a substance treatment program if required to do so. A sanctioned individual or family would still be entitled to Medicaid but not to any increase in other assistance programs (such as food stamps or housing assistance).

WRA would tighten penalties for any refusal to accept a bona fide offer of unsubsidized employment of at least twenty hours per week. Instead of the parent losing her share, the entire family would be off AFDC for six months or until the parent accepted employment. There would be penalties for violating the specific WORK requirements—refusal to report for an assignment, voluntarily leaving a position, refusal to engage in job search, and being discharged for misconduct. Sanctions would escalate from a 50 percent reduction in the family's AFDC benefits for the first failure to the fourth, and for any and all subsequent failures, the family would be totally cut off for six months.

Procedures to deal with disputes would be streamlined. For example, it appears as though arbitration or mediation rather than the more formal fair hearings would apply to disputes over the employability plan. Fair hearings would still be available for disputes over participation and sanctions.

The WRA contains provisions for increasing JOBS funding. States would be rewarded if their JOBS participation rate exceeded 55 percent and penalized if the rate fell below 45 percent. Those counting as JOBS participants would include only PIs, those employed at the minimum state level (twenty or, at state option, thirty hours per week), and—significantly—those who are under sanction. In other words, a state could meet its participation rate goals, and thus avoid federal penalties, by sanctioning more recipients.[17]

The estimated costs of the Work and Responsibility Act of 1994 are expected to be $9.3 billion over the first five years. The Clinton administration plans to finance these costs by reducing money spent in other programs, primarily benefit programs for the poor—for example, reducing the Emergency Assistance to Families Program by $1.6 billion, limiting eligibility for noncitizens for public assistance for an additional savings of $3.7 billion, cutting $800 million from Supplemental Security Income (SSI) by restricting disability benefits for substance abuse, and eliminating $3.2 billion from other programs, such as the Family Day Care Food Program.

The Republicans' PRA work requirements are considerably more stringent than the WRA's. In general, nonexempt recipients would be subject to a "transition component" for up to twenty-four months; thereafter, it would be the "work component." Under the transition component, states would be required to provide job search programs and would be prohibited from providing "subsidized non-work activities" (that is, education and training) for more than twenty-four months. This is a lifetime restriction, with no exceptions. States would also have the option of requiring workfare for one of the two years. The recipient would be required to work for a public or nonprofit agency for the welfare grant (Community Work Experience, CWEP), or the grant could be given to an employer who would then hire the recipient, or the recipient could participate in another federally approved work program. The recipient would be required to work for thirty-five hours per week, thirty hours if participating in a job search. States would only be *allowed* to provide CWEP for three years; they would have the option of cutting off welfare after only two years. But in either event, states could permanently terminate AFDC for the family even though the parent was unable to find a job.[18]

The experience of CWEP has thus far been very limited, but under the Republican bill, hundreds of thousands of job slots would have to be created. Typically, the parent in the CWEP slot receives only the AFDC grant. In the median state, with an AFDC grant of $367 for a family of three, thirty-five hours per week translates into $2.43 per hour. In Mississippi, where the AFDC grant is $120 per month, the "wage" is $.79 per hour. And in no state would the working parent qualify for unemployment, Social Security, or the EITC. Further, as noted, CWEP slots would be far more expensive for the states than simply providing welfare.

Under the PRA, states would be required to make a pro rata reduction in the family's monthly amount if the mother fails to meet the weekly thirty-five-hour work requirement. The reason would not matter—a child's illness, a family emergency—there are no exceptions for good cause.

Many more recipients would be required to participate in workfare under the PRA than under current law or the WRA. For example, the age of the youngest child would be lowered to six months (thus increasing child care costs). Mothers giving birth for the first time would be exempt for six months, with the months allocated before and after the birth; for subsequent children, only four months would be allowed. It is estimated that more than 80 percent of AFDC recipients would be required to participate under the Republican bill, as compared to about 43 percent under current law. This, of course, would increase the costs. The Congressional Budget Office estimated in 1993 that the cost of operating the flat thirty-five-hour-a-week slots in 1999 would be approximately $6,300 per slot. The House Republicans estimate that by 2001, 1.5 million recipients would be required to work under their bill, for a cost of more than $9 billion per year. This translates into costs of more than 40 percent per AFDC family in the median state.[19]

The Republican bill increases penalties on the families. For the first and second failures to comply, the family's AFDC and food stamps would be decreased by 25 percent until there is compliance; for the third failure, the family would lose AFDC permanently. If the first failure continues for more than a month, moreover, the family would move to the second failure, and if that continued for more than three months, the family would be treated as a three-strike failure. The bill provides neither for "good cause" excuses nor for opportunities to "cure" failures, such as the conciliation process provided under current law. Rather, penalties would apply to any failure to comply. Does this mean that a recipient who missed one appointment and failed to respond to two notices (perhaps misdelivered, perhaps the recipient changed addresses) would be ineligible for AFDC for life? Finally, even though the first and second penalties would removed when the individual complied, they would count toward a lifetime total of three.

The PRA increases state participation rates. Participants could only be counted if they met the flat thirty-five hours a week rule. For example, a recipient currently working for twenty-five hours per week would not count. Recipients who were supposed to work thirty-five hours per week but missed some days because of sickness or emergencies would also not count. Thus, many individuals would be working substantial hours but still would not "count" toward the required participation rate. Under the PRA, the initial participation rates are projected to be 2 percent of the AFDC caseload for FY 1996, 4 percent in FY 1997, 8 percent in FY 1998, 12 percent in FY 1999, and eventually 50 percent in FY 2003. The 2 percent rate translates into 100,000 persons; 12 percent, 600,000. In light of the JOBS experience, even the 2 percent figure is probably unrealistic. In FY 1992, fewer than 5 percent of JOBS participants—or less than .5 percent of AFDC recipients—would have been countable under the PRA.[20]

The workfare part of the Republican bill is obviously phony. Not only will it be impossible to implement a jobs program on this scale, but costs will have to increase considerably (the welfare grant plus the administration costs). Even more significant is that welfare recipients cannot live on their welfare grants alone. Recall Edin and Jencks's analysis of welfare families in Chicago (and replicated elsewhere). AFDC covered only about a third of living expenses; recipients obtained the rest primarily from work, mostly in the informal economy. If welfare recipients now have to work between thirty and thirty-five hours in a workfare job, they will not be able to supplement their income. Therefore, they will have to quit AFDC. Welfare will be "two years and you're out." This, of course, is a perfect solution for the Republicans. Extreme poverty may increase, but welfare rolls will shrink. Moreover, they will shrink, they will claim, under the threat of workfare.

Child Care

Whatever proposal is adopted—Democratic, Republican, or any of the states'—the legislation will have to face the significant issue of child care. Child care, including transitional care for those who take a job, is guaranteed under JOBS, and this guarantee would extend to those participating in WORK. The states would be allowed to set maximum payment allowances, but the allowances would have to be limited to the "market rate." Or, the states could use earnings disregards, limited to $200 a month for a child under two and $175 for all others; lesser amounts would be permitted if the parent were working part-time. There are no guarantees that these provisions will equal the actual cost of child care. In California, at least, the "market rate" is the rate for family-member child care.

Family-member day care has an intuitive appeal, with its friendly image of a grandmother rather than a stranger taking care of the children; it is cheaper than licensed care, and it is a way of employing additional poor families. But a recent study questions home-based day care by relatives. It turns out that quality of care is related more to training and, significantly, to commitments on the part of the child care providers. Low-income and minority children tended to receive lower quality care.[21]

And grandmothers, of course, are not always available. According to the Department of Labor, among employed mothers with children under five, 28 percent of employed mothers used child care centers and a third used family day-care homes. The results of a study of child care centers conducted by four universities in 1994 are even more disturbing. Researchers collected data from 826 children in fifty nonprofit and fifty for-profit randomly chosen centers in California, Colorado, Connecticut, and North Carolina. Their basic finding was that "child care at most centers in the United States is poor to mediocre, with almost half of the infants and toddlers in rooms having less than minimal quality." Minimal quality was defined as care that, although it met "basic health and safety needs," provided "little warmth and support" and "few learning experiences." Only one in seven centers was found to provide a level of care that "promotes healthy development and learning," the kind of warm relationships whereby children learn the trust and intellectual development necessary for school. Not surprisingly, the quality of child care was related to resources—staff-to-child ratios, staff education, training, and experience, and staff wages (97 percent female, with wages lower than even other female-dominated occupations). Center child care is expensive—again, as compared to welfare. Even mediocre care averaged ninety-five dollars per week per child. The centers provided the services that the parents needed. They met basic health and safety needs, and they were open long hours. The parents, however, overestimated the quality of care their children were receiving. Although 90 percent of parents rated the programs as "very good," trained observers rated the same programs "poor to mediocre."[22]

Under the PRA, child care costs are bound to increase because of the flat thirty-five-hour rule and the increased required participation rates. Yet the legislation contains no provisions to increase child care expenditures.

The Likely Outcomes of the Work Requirements

In assessing these so-called welfare reforms—whether Democratic or Republican—it must be emphasized that none do anything about the seriously inadequate levels of AFDC benefits or, for that matter, the extent of poverty in America. As noted, benefit levels have declined by 45 percent in the past two decades and now average $373 nationwide, which is a bit more than a third of what it takes a family of three to live on per month. Welfare families, on average, live at about two-thirds of the poverty line, but almost two-thirds of their income derives from other sources. The proposals not only fail to address this problem but also do nothing to prevent further erosion by the states. In fact, as discussed in chapter 5, the Clinton administration approved a California waiver to institute across-the-board cuts.

Nor will WORK requirements do much to relieve poverty. At minimum wage, if a parent worked the minimum requirement of twenty hours per week, the monthly earnings would be $368.02, or 45 percent of the poverty line for a family of two and 36 percent of the poverty line for a family of three. If the parent worked thirty hours per week, the monthly earnings would be $552.08, or 67 percent of the poverty line for a family of two and 54 percent of the poverty line for a family of three.[23] Given the low level of AFDC benefits and the likely earnings of the recipients, the administration is not interested in reducing poverty. The goal of the WRA is "self-sufficiency," but *self-sufficiency is defined as AFDC ineligibility* rather than a decent standard of living.

Because a twenty-four-month time clock with required subsidized employment has never been tried on a state or county level, let alone nationwide, no one knows what will happen. What we can do is point to some numbers, administrative issues, and experience to make some educated speculations. Accordingly, I first describe the numbers of recipients, or the magnitude of the problem. Second, I discuss the federal incentives and penalties vis-à-vis the states. The relevance of these provisions is that in the past, when states and counties have been faced with difficult conflicting policy and administrative demands, they have managed somehow to defer or deflect the pressures. With past work programs, it will be recalled, large numbers of registrants were put on administrative hold. Proposed legislation seeks to restrict this option through incentives and penalties on the states. Last, I analyze the likely consequences—for the states and counties and for the recipients.

When David Ellwood first proposed time-limited welfare with a guaranteed job for those recipients who could not find an unsubsidized job, he admitted that he did not know how many recipients would fall into this category, but he speculated that it would be a "tiny" number.[24] The number is still unknown, but one can be fairly certain that it will not be tiny. Recall that the highest employment impacts for a broad-based mandatory welfare-work program have been the GAIN program in Riverside County, California. Even in Riverside, however, at the end of three years, more than 40 percent of those subject to the GAIN requirements were still receiving AFDC. Under the WRA, WORK participants will be even poorer, since they will not qualify for the EITC. In Riverside, moreover, during the course of the three years, many more participants were employed but lost their jobs and needed to go back on welfare than kept jobs and stayed off welfare.

It also seems unlikely that a substantial number of recipients who have completed the two years of education and training will find an unsubsidized job. As discussed, from time immemorial welfare policy has assumed that there are sufficient jobs in the market for those who need them, but are there enough jobs that pay a living wage as compared to the number of people who are looking for those jobs? Curiously, the federal government has never systematically collected data on job vacancies. There have, however, been a number of studies comparing unemployment with vacancies. Reviewing these studies, Gordon Lafer has concluded that the "unemployed population significantly outweighs the number of job openings available at any point in time." Not surprisingly, the unemployment-to-vacancy rate increases along with the unemployment rate. With an unemployment rate of 5 percent, there were between three and four officially unemployed persons for every job vacancy.[25] And this means the officially unemployed—not the discouraged worker or the part-time worker who would like a full-time job. Philip Harvey has estimated that if these additional adults are included, then in New York City, in 1991, when the unemployment rate was about 9.3 percent, the number of people for every available job increases from approximately 7.7 to 10.9 persons.[26] And, of course, the ratio will increase if a couple of million

AFDC recipients entered the labor market. If the focus is on needy people who want living-wage jobs, then the ratios are even higher. For example, in an analysis of job opportunities in New York City in 1989, there were 777,000 economically disadvantaged adults and 57,000 job vacancies, or, as Lafer notes, about thirteen needy adults for every available job. Finally, the data show that there are not enough jobs to provide work for everyone who is actively seeking work in good times as well as bad. According to Harvey, when the unemployment rate was about 4.5 percent in the mid-1960s, there were approximately 2.5 unemployed persons for every vacant job. In 1982, conversely, with an unemployment rate of 9.5 percent, there were about 8.4 persons for every vacant job.

Gary Burtless speculates that over the long haul the U.S. labor market could absorb the extra millions of those seeking work. The reason that the labor market can do this, however, is that employers eventually shift production to accommodate an influx of low-wage workers. As he notes, for example, "Restaurant meals [are] prepared and served by 11th graders and high school dropouts rather than experienced cooks or waiters." The analogy is that if two million AFDC recipients were forced to accept private-sector jobs, most would eventually find them. But the inflow of unskilled workers would depress the wages received by other less skilled workers.[27]

Burtless is talking about the long run. In the short run, it seems likely that a substantial number of recipients will complete the two years but will still be unable to find an unsubsidized job. What will the states do? In an apparently unique move, Riverside County instituted a significant job development program, which took a tremendous administrative effort on the part of the agency leadership *and* did not consider nonwelfare job seekers. Even so, only about a third of Riverside participants got jobs, and most remained on welfare.

Realistically, it would be hard to replicate Riverside. Staff morale is always problematic. County social welfare departments are not employment agencies. The staff is primarily lower-level eligibility workers who are seriously overburdened normal case loads. The most difficult people to place are young, single mothers, who present the greatest problems in terms of making a stable connection to the labor force. And it is because these women have multiple employment barriers that they are projected to be longer-term recipients.

State Incentives and Sanctions

The proposed welfare reforms raise required participation rates, increase demands and sanctions on the participants, and do nothing about labor markets. Recall that under prior welfare-to-work programs, states resolved the conflicts between legislative demands and the costs of dealing with uncontrollable local labor markets by deferring or otherwise excusing large numbers of potential registrants. The WRA contains extensive and novel provisions designed to change state practices. Whether these or similar provisions survive depends on how the issue of state authority is resolved. If maximum authority is delegated to the states to run welfare as they see fit, then issues of incentives and sanctions will be minimal. However, to the extent that the federal government does seek to impose requirements, then incentives and sanctions become relevant. I assume here that there will be at least some federal requirements, even with block grants.

The WRA attempts to control state practices of deferring recipients by providing that states could place only an additional 5 percent (increasing to 10 percent in FY 1999) of mandatory registrants in the deferral category for "other" criteria. This permitted increase is to cover "good cause" reasons, such as learning disabilities or emotional problems. States could petition for an increase in the good cause cap "based on extraordinary circumstances." If the cap were exceeded, the federal government would reduce its share of AFDC grants by 25 percent for the people who exceeded the cap. States would be rewarded for having participation rates exceeding 55 percent of the mandatory group and could be penalized for having a participation rate that falls below 45 percent. The penalty would involve a reduction in the federal match for the cost of the basic AFDC grant multiplied by the number of cases by which the state failed to meet the applicable standard.[28]

Will these penalties increase recipient participation? Prior experience should help us answer this question. First, there is the experience of federal penalties vis-à-vis the states under the federal quality control system. Starting in the late 1960s (when the demographic characteristics of AFDC had changed and the rolls and costs had expanded), there arose serious political concerns about "waste, fraud, and abuse" in welfare. The federal government imposed quality-control requirements on the states.[29] If the states exceeded a certain "error rate"—a percentage of active files with errors—federal penalties were to be imposed. Cases were monitored by both federal and state governments for errors.[30]

Two things happened that are relevant for our purposes. As a result of great pressure, there was a dramatic tightening of administrative requirements, and local agencies developed the practice of "churning." Rather than risk errors, workers closed cases for relatively harmless procedural errors. AFDC entails an enormous number of forms and documents: Social Security numbers for children, birth certificates, address confirmations, verifications of work requirements, failures to keep appointments, and so forth.[31] Procedural rejections of applications increased almost 50 percent between 1972 and 1984; procedural terminations rose from 14 percent of all closings in 1972 to 41 percent in 1984. Most (but not all) were restored when the procedural error was cured.[32]

The second thing that happened was that in spite of states' efforts, they still exceeded federal caps, and substantial penalties were imposed. By 1983, it was estimated that states' total financial liabilities would reach $3 billion in 1989.[33] Rather than pay the penalties, however, the states sued the federal government. Congress commissioned a study, and as far as I know, the government collected few if any fines.[34] The lesson is that when it comes to contests between the states and the federal government, the states usually win.

But a strange thing happened. Even though the states were able to avoid federal sanctions, they succeeded in enforcing quality control on their own. Although the states could not conform to the unreasonably strict requirements imposed by the federal government, it was to their fiscal advantage to tighten up on administrative waste and reduce welfare costs by enforcing strict rules—what Michael Lipsky has called "bureaucratic disentitlement."[35]

This experience may or may not be relevant depending on how much authority is ultimately delegated to the states and what federal requirements will apply. Under the WRA, if the states exceed the 5 percent good cause deferral rate or the 10 percent extension rate, they will be sanctioned—just like exceeding the quality-control error rate. If these were the only factors involved, then one would predict the same result—namely, that in the end the states would not pay substantial fines to the federal government.

The WRA penalty structure for recipients could change the equation. Families who were sanctioned would be counted as "participants" for the purposes of the deferral and extension rates. In addition, the sanctions would be considerably more severe than under prior programs. Until the WRA, only the adult offender lost her portion of the AFDC grant; now it would be the entire family—at first a 50 percent reduction and then a 100 percent reduction—for a six-month period. There would now be two incentives for the state to sanction—one, it would help them with the federal caps on deferral and extensions, and two, it would increase their savings. Under prior rules, where only the adult offender lost her grant, there was more of a balance between the administrative costs of imposing a sanction and the savings; now, the savings would be increased substantially. AFDC, JOBS, and WORK are complicated programs, with pages of requirements. There are countless ways in which recipients can be excused or sanctioned: the bus was late, a doctor's note did not arrive on time, a job search verification was not filed, an appointment was missed. As noted, under quality control, states were willing to close thousands of cases on procedural errors. Now, they might be able to save as much as $2,500 per case for a six-month sanction.[36]

Yet sanctions can be counterproductive. The WRA assumes that sanctions are needed to send a "message"—that the work requirements should be taken seriously. Actually, there is little evidence that welfare recipients need a message; the most credible evidence in fact points the other way. We have seen in the empirical research that the great majority of welfare recipients are not long term and that most eventually leave welfare via work. The problems are the lack of adequate jobs, day care, and health benefits, not the work ethic. It is also true that in the more successful programs—even in Riverside County—sanctions are few and are downplayed. The strong emphasis, rather, is on cooperation and support between staff and recipients and the provision of services. The failure of a recipient is considered a staff and agency failure, too.

Finally, as Yeheskel Hasenfeld's research has shown, it is hard for an agency to combine sanctions with work programs.[37] Agencies that employ sanctions are bureaucratic, rule-oriented, rigid, and distant from clients. They substitute rules for the intensive, time-consuming strategy of patiently working with clients that need help. These agencies experience far less compliance than agencies that downplay sanctions. Alameda County, which has an inner-city, potentially long-term clientele, also has the highest number of recipients in the better jobs and runs, in effect, a voluntary program. Yet, the WRA would mandate incentives to make sanctions more important. This would not only not increase employment but would significantly increase hardship.

This last point—the increase in hardship—may blunt the incentives to sanction. Under quality-control sanctions, many families (but not all) get back on welfare within a relatively short time. Under the WRA, the penalty would last at least six months. Although states have been willing to let AFDC benefits decline gradually or impose small percentage cuts (especially since food stamps would rise with the cost of living), they have been less willing to impose wholesale cut-offs on a large scale. General Relief can be cut; single adults will drift and die slowly, usually out of sight. Families with children are different. States and counties can go only so far in reducing grants before families become homeless and show up in shelters, before there are increased demands for emergency assistance and private charity, and children must be placed in foster care. In addition to increasing hardship, these alternatives are usually much more costly than AFDC both politically and fiscally for states and local governments. Foster care costs vary by state. In some high-benefit states, foster care may not be much more expensive than AFDC. But in many states it is more than twice as costly. In Illinois—the median state—AFDC for a family of three costs $367 per month; foster care for two children costs $637, or 73.6 percent more.[38] Thus, it is not clear how stringently sanctions will be imposed in spite of current attempts to close lower-level loopholes and to increase state incentives to impose sanctions.

Changing Social Behavior

Both the Democratic and Republican proposals, and many of the state reforms, deal with "family values." Some reforms could be helpful; most are regulatory and punitive. The federal government continues to increase enforcement for child support. The WRA provides for a further streamlining of the process, strengthens requirements for updating awards, establishes a commission to study whether national support guidelines should be adopted, establishes federal and state registries to improve collections, and improves the process by which families receive amounts collected.

Conversely, all of the reforms increase the requirements on the mother to cooperate in establishing paternity. In FY 1992, paternity had not been established for almost 30 percent—2.8 million—of all AFDC children. Large numbers could lose eligibility. Under the PRA, states would be required to deny assistance where paternity has not been established except in cases where the child was conceived as a result of rape or incest or the state determines that efforts to establish paternity would result in physical danger to the mother. Under the WRA, the mother would have not only to identify the father but also to provide such verifiable information as addresses, date of birth, and names of relatives to enable the state to locate the father. The agency that determines whether the mother is complying would be in charge of child support enforcement, rather than the welfare agency. In many states, this decision would be made by law enforcement agencies that have contracted out paternity establishment and support enforcement. If the mother did not provide sufficient information—the father's name and address or his immediate relatives—the entire family would be denied aid. Under the PRA, even if the mother fully cooperated, she would receive no assistance while the state was trying to locate the absent father or if the father could not be located. If she failed to comply, the family would lose her share of the grant. The state agencies (welfare and child support enforcement) would be responsible for developing "good cause" regulations in terms of the child's best interests.

Under the PRA, states would be required to deny aid permanently to a child born out of wedlock to a mother younger than eighteen (or at the states' option, twenty-one), unless the mother subsequently marries the father or the child is adopted out. This is a lifetime disqualification, even if the child went to live with another relative. This means that if a child is born to a single woman who is less than eighteen or (at state option) twenty-one years old, and then, say, five years later, the mother loses her job, that child would still not receive AFDC. States could use any savings for residential homes for unwed mothers, orphanages, programs to reduce out-of-wedlock pregnancies, and so forth, but not for abortions or abortion counseling.

States would be required to impose the family cap unless they specifically exempted themselves. The PRA would require states to deny assistance to any child born to an AFDC recipient and to any child born to an individual who received AFDC at any time during the ten-month period ending with the birth of the child. This would include a child in utero if the mother was on AFDC—that child would be barred from AFDC when born.

Proposals for teen parents also go both ways. Funding for pregnancy prevention programs is authorized to increase to $100 million by FY 1999. Under present law, states could require minor AFDC parents to live in the home of their parents or other responsible adults. To date, only five states have taken this option, probably because most teen parents already live at home or have good reason not to. Nevertheless, current proposals would change the option to a requirement. There are safeguards to prevent, for example, danger to the teen parent or the child, and a case manager would be assigned to each minor custodial parent.

Other proposals would strengthen Learnfare programs. Both penalties and rewards would be permitted.

States could provide lower benefits to new residents (the benefits would be based on the state of origin). At present, this provision is unconstitutional, but the Supreme Court has recently agreed to reconsider the issue.

Ending Entitlement Status and Capping Spending

"Responsibility" has replaced "entitlement." Accordingly, there are various proposals to end AFDC as an "entitlement" by capping spending and/or folding AFDC, along with other aid programs, into block grants to the states. Under present law, all who meet eligibility requirements are required to be enrolled; state and federal funding are open-ended. This is what is meant by an "entitlement." With spending capped, with or without a block grant, when the money runs out, no more eligible applicants would be enrolled. This is what happened when state and local welfare funds were exhausted during the Depression. What would happen under current proposals is not known at present. Federal grants may be capped, but there may very well be entitlements under state law, which of course worries state governors, since these "additional" recipients would be 100 percent financed with state dollars. Or states could repeal their entitlements, in which event the burden would fall on other programs (such as foster care) or on counties and localities.

Under the PRA, the programs that would be included in the block grant are AFDC, AFDC work program, Child Support Enforcement, At-Risk Child Care, Supplemental Security Income (SSI), and fifteen housing programs (including public housing and Section 8). AFDC, SSI, Child Support Enforcement, and At-Risk Child Care would lose entitlement status. Effective FY 1996, the amount of federal spending for the block could not exceed the estimated spending for the previous year, adjusted for inflation for the most recent fiscal year and for changes in the poverty population for three years earlier. The bill contains a provision for states to opt out of AFDC altogether, as Wisconsin has announced that it intends to do. In this case, the state would receive a block grant (slightly more than what they would receive under AFDC for FY 1992) to administer "any program established by the State to provide benefits to needy families with dependent children." States would be required to file an annual accounting report, and the Department of Health and Human Services could reduce the state grant by up to 20 percent if funds were not spent properly.

Under any of these scenarios, the states will be at considerable risk. If there was a recession, either nationally or locally, Congress would be under no duty to provide additional funds; the poor would have to compete with other claimants. Moreover, the poverty "adjuster" would be calculated on the basis of the poverty rate several years earlier. That is, spending for assistance would be based not on present need but on need three years earlier. And changes in the poverty rate might not reflect demographic changes—for example, more elderly people needing SSI or more children needing AFDC.

States run similar risks if they opt for the block grant. The block grant is to be fixed at 103 percent of FY 1994 funding, but there are no provisions for need adjustments that might be caused by recessions, demographic changes, or population increases. Furthermore, as we have seen, if a state wanted to increase the work effort of AFDC recipients, it would have to incur increased up-front costs. Just about any welfare-to-work program is more expensive than straight welfare. And the current version of the WRA proposal contains strict penalties for the states. If the secretary of HHS were to determine that the states spent "any amount" for purposes other than the program for needy families with children, the secretary would be required to reduce the state's allocation by 20 percent. In addition, because AFDC would no longer be an entitlement, states could not be sure that they would even get the 103 percent year after year. Finally, there would still be federal restrictions on the block grant. For example, even with the block grants, states would be prohibited from giving aid to children born to welfare mothers, children born to mothers under eighteen out of wedlock, and so forth.

Denial of Assistance to Legal Immigrants

Only citizens are eligible for the major assistance programs—AFDC, Food Stamps, SSI, Medicaid—as well as many other programs. Under the PRA, with few exceptions, legal immigrants would also be ineligible for sixty federally assisted programs.[39] The great bulk of the savings—estimated by the Republicans at $22 billion—would come from the denial of nonemergency Medicaid and SSI.

Again, the impact would fall on the states. Denying federal assistance does not make poor immigrants or poor families with children disappear. They will still be elderly, blind, disabled, sick. They will still need care. Immigrant children will still need child protection services, immunizations, and health screening. In many states, statutes will provide that assistance. But under the PRA, the funds will be entirely state and local dollars rather than federal cost-sharing.

Criminal justice and welfare reform have an eerie similarity today. Fear and frustration have turned the focus of criminal law to deterrence and retribution. The reinstitution of the death penalty and establishment of "three strikes and you're out" laws at the state level are also symbolic assertions of control, to make law-abiding citizens feel somehow that they are in control, even though neither measure will much affect crime. Welfare reform is proceeding along the same path. In the elections of 1992, the "new" Democrats tried to make sense of the new mood in the nation, the growing insistence on work rather than on dependence. They needed a message to show that they were serious, so they proposed the simplistic concept of time-limited welfare. This would show the voters that they really were going to "end welfare as a way of life." But in so doing, the Democrats have trapped themselves into an impossible, palpably unworkable welfare-to-work scheme. No one is going to pay the costs of subsidized work for these kinds of numbers; so there are phase-in groups, excuses, loopholes, and subsidies for those who could not find employment. The message, however, rather than retreating, became reality. The Republicans have adopted time-limited welfare but without providing jobs or income. Several states are not far behind Wisconsin and Massachusetts: welfare is becoming "two years and you're out." Like criminal law reform, the new phase of welfare reform will solve nothing. Jobs will not be available, certainly in the required numbers. Families will be poorer—which was the trend anyway—and life will go on much as before, subject to larger changes in society.

7 Another Exercise in Symbolic Politics

To show how quickly and how far welfare policy has moved to the right, we return to the Clinton administration's initial plans, formulated as recently as 1992. Although the administration did introduce time-limited welfare, its programs for the poor have contained much more, including the much needed expansion of the Earned Income Tax Credit, which has been enacted, proposed increases in the minimum wage, and plans for universal affordable health care. These measures are much broader than welfare; they address the poverty and near-poverty conditions of the working poor. But because so many welfare recipients are in and out of paid employment, trying to make permanent connections with the labor market, enactment of these provisions would go a long way toward reducing welfare dependency. The administration has also proposed increasing efforts to ensure parental child support, expanding child care and Head Start, and instituting special health programs for women and children. All of the liberals who adopted a tough work requirement emphasized education, training, and, most important, increasing the returns from private sector employment. It is no secret that welfare rolls rise and fall with employment rates.

Yet, in an important sense, when it came time to make tough political decisions, the Democrats experienced a failure of nerves. Once again, following history, they separated the working poor—the worthy poor—from the welfare (unworthy) poor, thereby perpetuating the stigma of welfare. The Clinton administration's welfare proposals are said to be based on the work of David Ellwood, but there are crucial differences. In his book *Poor Support,* Ellwood proposed making work pay by expanding the EITC, raising the minimum wage, and providing health care and child care benefits. In addition, Ellwood proposed a $2,000 annual child support guarantee per child if fathers failed to pay. And his plan would require the mother to work only half-time, arguing that it is unreasonable and unwise to expect a single mother, especially of young children, to be both a full-time worker and a mother. The majority of nonwelfare mothers, though in the paid labor force, choose not to be full-time workers. Ellwood argues that working half-time at a minimum-wage job, with an expanded EITC, plus health benefits, day care, and guaranteed child support would bring a single mother about up to the poverty line. If she wanted greater income, she would work more, but the choice would be hers. Ellwood does call for an end to welfare for the able-bodied. Welfare should be transitional, with single mothers either finding private sector (half-time) jobs or the government providing jobs, which, as noted, Ellwood speculates would be a small number.[1]

Two things are striking. First, the Clinton administration, in addition to abandoning proposals to raise the minimum wage (only recently revived), dropped two of the most important parts of Ellwood's reform plan—*half-time work and guaranteed child support*—out of its own welfare reform plan (there were provisions for a few guaranteed child support demonstration projects). The administration endorsed health care and subsidized work (the EITC) for the working poor, but, it will be recalled, specified that EITC would not apply to WORK jobs. Second, the only aspects of both Ellwood's and Clinton's plans that have become popular are the two-year cut-off and required work. The opportunity for an inclusive antipoverty debate was lost.

The Strange Silence of the Earned Income Tax Credit

The symbolic importance given to time-limited welfare is illustrated by the administration's silence regarding the Earned Income Tax Credit. The expansion of the EITC under the Clinton administration is clearly one of the most important antipoverty income transfer measures to have been enacted in a generation. When fully funded, it will pull about fourteen million working poor families out of poverty. Yet it is almost never mentioned in terms of welfare reform.

Three crucial changes have been made in the Earned Income Tax Credit: (1) it now applies to welfare recipients; previously, at least 50 percent of a person's income had to be from "earnings," which excluded recipients; (2) benefits have been raised significantly; and (3) EITC receipts are not counted against welfare income.

How these changes came about and their importance for AFDC recipients is little known. When Richard M. Nixon's Family Assistance Plan was defeated in the 1970s, Senator Russell Long, no friend of welfare, introduced the EITC to help the working poor. Consistent with historic traditions of separating welfare recipients from the working poor, welfare recipients were not eligible even if they worked. A working parent had to have a legal dependent *and* provide more than half the support through earnings. It turned out that the earnings requirement caused a lot of errors, and in the late 1970s, the Internal Revenue Service lobbied to have that requirement dropped and to replace it with eligibility based only on legal dependents. But the true conservatives in the Reagan administration passed a number of AFDC reforms designed to strengthen the distinction between the working poor and welfare recipients and accordingly refused the IRS's request. The Bush administration didn't care. The 50 percent requirement was dropped. This meant that AFDC mothers who worked would now be eligible. The Clinton administration made additional changes. The amount of the credit was significantly increased, and the credit was not deducted from welfare benefits.

The EITC is now a significant income transfer program. Nearly fourteen million families now receive the credit; when fully funded, the program will amount to more than $7 billion a year. And it enjoys strong bipartisan support. For individual families, it is a substantial payback. For a family with two or more children, earning $8,500 per year, the benefit is $3,370 (39.7 percent), which places that family at just about the poverty line. When the EITC is fully phased in, in 1996, the credit rate will be 40 percent of earnings for families with two or more children (with a maximum credit of $3,370) and 34 percent for families with one child (with a maximum of $2,040).[2] For families with two or more children, the expanded EITC will increase the earnings from a minimum-wage job to $5.95 per hour. More than six million working families with incomes below the poverty line will be eligible for benefits, and the poverty gap will be decreased by $6.4 billion.[3]

To illustrate the effects of the EITC on a welfare family, we can use the working welfare mothers who participated in Eden and Jencks's study as examples. These women had jobs that paid about $5 an hour. If a mother worked twenty-five hours per week for forty-eight weeks at $5 per hour, she would earn $6,000 and receive about $2,400 in EITC. The total, $8,400, is $3,600 more than she would get for her family in Illinois (AFDC and Food Stamps come to $4,800 a year). The EITC is not trouble-free—indeed, there are important problems of program integrity.[4] Still, it is a significant measure for the working poor.

With a majority of welfare recipients already working, more than two-thirds of them exiting welfare via work, and the changes in the EITC sure to accelerate that process, one would think that the

EITC expansion would be at the center of welfare reform. Instead, it is barely mentioned. The reasons why tell us a lot about the symbolism of welfare reform.

The EITC was conceived and developed as a distinct *alternative* to welfare reform. The proposed Family Assistance Plan would have helped both the working poor and the welfare recipient. During debate on the FAP, conservatives essentially told liberals that if they wanted to help the working poor, then they should do it directly—and there was bipartisan support for the EITC. That support has continued as long as EITC has been considered help for the working poor, continuing the historic distinction between the worthy and unworthy poor. And today, even though EITC will substantially help working welfare recipients, it is different from welfare. For example, whereas under welfare, the more a person earns, the more welfare is reduced, with the EITC, benefits *increase* as earnings increase, up to a specified cut-off. That is, EITC is tied directly to gainful employment. Although it now helps welfare recipients, it helps only those who behave like the working poor—the more they work, the more benefits they will receive. The EITC subsidizes those who are working. It makes paid employment more attractive to those who are out of work. Unfortunately, it does not create jobs.

To attach the EITC politically to welfare reform would probably cause a decline in its bipartisan support. Conservatives are already noticing its significant transfer effects, as well as its error rates, and they are, predictably, beginning to raise objections.[5] Similar approaches to separate the working poor from the welfare poor can be detected in the Clinton administration's failed efforts to reform health care and the current effort to raise the minimum wage. There is debate about the antipoverty effects of raising the minimum wage—some argue that a higher minimum wage would reduce low-wage employment opportunities and that a great many minimum wage workers are not in poor families—but most policymakers concede that a modest increase would be beneficial. And there is no credible argument against the proposition that extending health coverage to the low-wage market is crucial in reducing welfare dependency. Yet welfare reform is barely mentioned in these debates.

The fact that EITC, as well as health care reform and the minimum wage hike, has to be kept separate from welfare reform in the political debates illustrates how little Americans have progressed in our thinking about welfare. These provisions attack the welfare problem where it should be—the labor market. They try to "make work pay." Instead, with welfare reform, both the Democrats and the Republicans, reflecting the "consensus," continue to concentrate on threatening and punishing those outside the labor market. It is the same old tactic of deterrence, of holding the welfare recipient hostage to the working poor.

The Future

How will all of this be sorted out? David Ellwood and Mary Jo Bane, shortly before they joined the Clinton administration, published a book in which they argued that the Family Support Act of 1988 was now considered to be either an "irrelevance or a failure."[6] Why? Although the FSA did stress work, education, and training, it failed to change the culture of welfare from "eligibility-compliance" to "self-sufficiency." Welfare still viewed work as an condition of eligibility rather than as a route out of poverty. Welfare offices were focused on compliance with rules; clients were adversaries. And a working client would be "error prone." Counter models were Massachusetts's ET and the Riverside County GAIN programs. Why? In Massachusetts, in addition to state and local political support and resources (and tight labor markets), client participation was voluntary; this meant, write the authors, that the workers "had to sell the program and invest themselves" in order to get the client committed. This is the self-sufficiency culture. They interpret Riverside as a total commitment on the part of management and workers. There were sanctions in Riverside, but "good management . . . appears to require playing down the mandatory aspects in order to motivate workers, circumvent legalistic interpretation of rules, and avoid relying on sanctions as client motivators."[7]

Welfare reform today—every proposal—is an about-face. Massachusetts's ET program is the polar opposite of the WRA, PRA, Wisconsin, and new Massachusetts legislation. Instead of a resource-rich, tight labor market, *voluntary* expensive program that emphasized higher up-front, short-term costs, welfare-to-work is a phased-in, short-funded program that relies more on quick job search and tough sanctions. ET imposed no time limits and no sanctions. Riverside County's GAIN program focuses on job search and quick entry into the labor market and it does impose sanctions. But the unique features of Riverside are its charismatic leadership, the total administrative reorganization of the agency, strong worker-client commitments, services to employed clients, the crucial importance of job development, the realistic acceptance of the need for work *and* welfare, and the distinct downplaying of sanctions. Again, this hardly describes today's reforms. The new reformers' changes to the culture of welfare are more in the direction of General Relief—a short period of assistance and then you're out.

It is also typical of Washington hubris to talk about changing the culture of a program such as AFDC. If just one thing is clear from the history of AFDC, it is that there is no national program. There are not even fifty state programs. Rather, many crucial decisions are discretionary determinations made in hundreds, perhaps thousands of local welfare offices. Moreover, trends toward increasing decentralization have accelerated. It is in these local offices that individual workers and their immediate supervisors will determine who is "making sufficient progress toward self-sufficiency," when to excuse, when to refer, when to defer, and when to sanction. Local officials will determine who is deserving and who is not. Relief for those who fit into morally problematic categories has always been decided this way. Anyone who is at least passingly familiar with complex organizations knows that this kind of field-level decisionmaking is exceedingly hard to monitor or to change. The culture of welfare may change someday, but not because of another wave of under-funded legislation from Washington that continues the tradition of delegating most of the important decisions to state and local governments.

I have argued that the "new" welfare reforms are not really new but rather continuations of the same old attitudes about the nature and causes of poverty and, basically, the same old remedies. This, of course, is especially true for the Republican proposals and the Wisconsin and Massachusetts legislation—the cut-off for adults even if no workfare slots materialize, the denial of aid for children conceived while the mother was on welfare or where paternity cannot be established or where one of the parents is a teen. Basically, then, we can expect the same results. As under prior work programs, some recipients will get jobs and some will be sanctioned, but the vast majority will somehow be deferred and life will go on. Their lives will improve only when the economy improves.

Will the two-year cut-off make a difference? As I have stated, this, too, is the old, cheap remedy that is now being applied with General Relief. Will the states be serious about this cut-off with welfare recipients? Will they follow Wisconsin's and Massachusetts's lead? They might, but this is not certain, at least with many welfare families. The new sanction provisions could make a difference, but only marginally, I expect. Politicians find it easier to cut off General Relief than AFDC. Punishing welfare mothers also punishes children, and we have not reached the point where we treat children as harshly as we do single able-bodied men and women. Mothers and children show up in shelters, and children arrive in foster homes and institutions. These systems are already overburdened, the expenses to the public are greater than for AFDC, and the outcomes for children in foster care are problematic. Moreover, more often than not, these programs are paid for with state and county dollars. For both fiscal and humanitarian reasons, we cannot push families as far as single adults.

Under this line of reasoning, one could argue that it would be better to encourage even *more* state control over AFDC. The reasoning is as follows: As a result of the elections in 1994, we have seen the

House Republicans insisting on even tougher federal AFDC requirements but without paying the costs. Until the very recent legislative change, the federal government had increasingly resorted to the practice of mandating state requirements without putting up the money.[8] In spite of the new law that purportedly prohibits unfunded mandates, the House Republicans now say that the states will pay for whatever increased costs are associated with welfare savings (such as foster care, shelters, and health care), but this is chimerical. In chapter 6, we saw the differences between AFDC and foster care. With increasing federal control, therefore, we can expect harder welfare sanctions to serve the political needs of national-level politicians who are not responsible for the consequences. The states will have to pick up the pieces—with shelters, foster care, or, as some have suggested, orphanages. From the states' perspective, these alternatives are not preferable to AFDC. Aside from indicating even worse outcomes for children, these alternatives are more expensive in state dollars. In other words, state welfare reforms are constrained in ways that are not present at the federal level. It is no surprise that many Republican governors, along with Democratic governors, are decidedly unenthusiastic about the House Republicans welfare reform proposals.

This is not a firm conclusion—proposed legislation to close loopholes and increase the sanctions and rewards to states for compliance may alter the outcome. It is particularly significant that sanctioned recipients would both count toward state compliance goals and increase welfare savings to the states. In the end, however, I think that there are limits to how much harm society is willing to permit to poor mothers and their children.

If the past is any guide, the likely outcome of the current reform crisis is that the federal government and the states will enact all sorts of time-limited welfare and family value restrictions. Some recipients will proceed through the work and training programs and get jobs (whether as a result of the programs they are enrolled in is another matter). Some will be cut from welfare, and this will reduce welfare costs and increase hardship. Some babies will be denied assistance, and some mothers will not have additional children. Some teen mothers will graduate from high school and some will not. *Both* the small number who seem to conform to the new regime and the small number who are sanctioned will be trumpeted as "successes." But again, the overwhelming majority of recipients will somehow be deferred or excused. That has been the experience. If the economy continues to improve, welfare reform will begin to fade as an issue, much to the relief of state politicians. If the economy stagnates and high levels of economic insecurity remain, then welfare reform will continue to be a salient political issue, and we will go through yet another round of "reform."

What, then, is going on? Why the obsession with welfare reform? Politicians as well as the general population hold welfare reform a higher priority than health care reform, deficit reduction, or the economy. And although we have many social ills and lots of problems with families and children and crime and drugs, the problems of health care, deficit reduction, and the economy are much larger than those associated with welfare.

We continue to live in a world of symbolic politics. The stereotype of the nineteenth-century immigrant single mother living in sin, the gesture of the early mothers' pensions programs, the disdain for the underclass welfare mother of today are all symbols, less to "reform" the deviants than to make society feel good about itself. Majoritarian society affirms its norms by stigmatizing others. Punishing the deviants and rewarding the virtuous, even if few in number, is a ceremonial exercise for the myth of control.

The myth and ceremony of deviant control is a grave matter because it is so ubiquitous and enduring. Today's AFDC recipients suffer from so many negatively ascribed characteristics—African-American, sexual promiscuity, underclass, criminality, substance abuse, spawning a new generation of criminals—that one wonders whether attitudes will ever change. When we look at who these people actually are—single adults, trying to get off welfare, trying to raise their children, trying to make lives for themselves—and when we see these children growing up in such wretched conditions (and most of them succeeding), the cruelty of the persistent stereotype is overwhelming. The welfare stereotype is the Willie Horton of the nineties.

For decades conservatives have maintained consistent opinions about what causes and cures the phenomenon of poor single motherhood. What is new, and tragic, is that the liberals have now bought into this view. As noted, when Irwin Garfinkel, Sara McLanahan, and then David Ellwood proposed time-limited welfare, they coupled it with a strong array of work preparation services, guaranteed jobs, guaranteed child support, and other benefits. But Ellwood did insist that after two years, welfare should end. What happened was predictable. The conservatives, as well as most of the nation, seized on the time limits and paid only lip service to the other provisions. There was some talk about work preparation, but there has been no mention of the all-important guaranteed child support or guaranteed jobs at a higher minimum wage, and without these provisions, these families will remain in severe poverty.

Liberals seems to have short memories. More than two decades ago, liberals and conservatives joined forces in the movement to deinstitutionalize the mental health care system. The stated plan was for the large mental health institutions to be closed and the mentally ill to be brought home to community mental health care, which would both be better mental health practice and save money. And so the mentally ill came home, but the money for community mental health somehow never appeared. What happened to the mentally ill in communities throughout the nation was shameful.[9] Now, by joining the welfare reform "consensus," again liberals have failed to take account of long-standing harsh attitudes toward the poor and the weak.

Why does "ending welfare as we know it" through mandatory work requirements and cut-offs dominate the political discussion? Why are the other antipoverty measures, such as the EITC, health care, raising the minimum wage, child support, and expanded education *not* mentioned as part of welfare reform in the media and by politicians? Why do we insist on Learnfare and the family cap when there is no evidence that these are either problems or solutions?

It is our age-old practice to treat the dependent poor as different, deviant, in need of moral reform. The new paternalism, or "tough love," is not new. Even the wretched poorhouses were justified on rehabilitative terms. Then, reformers claimed that institutional confinement would extricate poor children from the baleful influence of the slums and they would learn good habits.[10] Times are hard and everyone is sore about welfare, about people not helping themselves, and once again the solution is to set the poor to work in spite of overwhelming evidence that work policies and programs generally fail to reduce welfare rolls in any appreciable way or improve the economic self-sufficiency of the poor. The evidence is consistent that the welfare poor share the work ethic and that most seize opportunities to improve themselves and leave welfare when they can. The evidence that sanctions are effective is inconclusive. None of the welfare programs, whether education, training, job search, or workfare, does anything to change the labor markets, and adequately paying jobs are becoming increasingly unavailable. "Welfare" as contrasted with "work" is simply an anachronistic idea for most single mothers on welfare. And yet policymakers and academics alike insist that we have to "send a message."

President Bill Clinton's initial instincts were correct—emphasize health care benefits, the value of private sector employment, and the Earned Income Tax Credit, and downplay welfare reform. "Making work pay" is the way to reduce the most important problem: poverty. Welfare rolls, hence costs, decline when adequately paying jobs are available. At that point, welfare programs can concentrate on the more troublesome cases. Welfare reform by itself does nothing to improve the job market, and unless there are more jobs that pay a higher income, we will have done nothing to lessen poverty or reduce welfare. And when we continue to do nothing about poverty, we continue to condemn the next generation. The research findings on the poor outcomes for children in foster care and cheap child care are truly disturbing. Welfare reformers profess great concern that welfare children are at risk of not growing up to become successful adults. The current consensus on welfare reform mocks that concern.

Notes

Chapter 1: Welfare and Poverty

1 Probably the most important statement is Lawrence Mead, *Beyond Entitlement: The Social Obligation of Citizenship* (New York: Free Press, 1986).
2 The idea of time-limited welfare was first put forward by Irwin Garfinkel and Sara McLanahan, *Single Mothers and Their Children: A New American Dilemma* (Washington, D.C.: Urban Institute Press, 1986), which was followed by David Ellwood, *Poor Support* (New York: Basic Books, 1988).
3 Gertrude Himmelfarb, *The Idea of Poverty: England in the Early Industrial Age* (New York: Vintage, 1983).
4 Michael B. Katz, "Introduction: The Urban 'Underclass' as a Metaphor of Social Transformation," in *The "Underclass" Debate*, ed. Michael B. Katz (Princeton, N.J.: Princeton University Press, 1993).
5 Karl de Schweinitz, *England's Road to Social Security, 1349–1947* (Philadelphia: University of Pennsylvania Press, 1947).

Chapter 2: The Past Is Prologue

Note to epigraph: Walter Trattner, *From Poor Law to Welfare State,* 4th ed. (New York: Free Press, 1989), 86.

1 Karl de Schweinitz, *England's Road to Social Security, 1349–1947* (Philadelphia: University of Pennsylvania Press, 1947).

2 De Schweinitz, *England's Road.*

3 De Schweinitz, *England's Road.*

4 Trattner, *From Poor Law to Welfare State,* 17.

5 Michael B. Katz, *In the Shadow of the Poorhouse* (New York: Basic Books, 1986).

6 Trattner, *From Poor Law to Welfare State,* 18–20.

7 Trattner, *From Poor Law to Welfare State,* 21.

8 Quoted in Gertrude Himmelfarb, *The Idea of Poverty: England in the Early Industrial Age* (New York: Vintage, 1983), 147–50.

9 Katz, *Shadow of the Poorhouse,* 11.

10 Trattner, *From Poor Law to Welfare State,* 17.

11 Trattner, *From Poor Law to Welfare State,* 49.

12 Himmelfarb, *Idea of Poverty,* 149.

13 Trattner, *From Poor Law to Welfare State,* 17–18.

14 *Report from His Majesty's Commissioners for Inquiring into the Administration and Practical Operation of the Poor Laws* (London, 1834), 148; Himmelfarb, *Idea of Poverty,* 165.

15 Quoted in Trattner, *From Poor Law to Welfare State,* 56.

16 "Letters to the Secretary of State on the Subject of Pauperism," *Columbia Republican* (1853), quoted in Katz, *Shadow of the Poorhouse,* 32.

17 Himmelfarb, *Idea of Poverty,* 175–76.

18 Trattner, *From Poor Law to Welfare State,* 55.

19 Charles Burroughs, "A Discourse Delivered in the Chapel of New Almshouse, in Portsmouth, N.H., Dec. 15, 1834, on the Occasion of Its First Being Opened for Religious Service," reprinted in David J. Rothman, ed., *The Jacksonians on the Poor: Collected Pamphlets* (New York: Arno Press, 1971), 3–10; Trattner, *From Poor Law to Welfare State,* 52–53.

20 Trattner, *From Poor Law to Welfare State,* 53.

21 Roy Lubove, "The New York Association for Improving the Condition of the Poor," *New-York Historical Quarterly* 43 (July 1959): 302–28.

22 Trattner, *From Poor Law to Welfare State,* 65–66.

23 Katz, *Shadow of the Poorhouse,* 41–42.

24 Trattner, *From Poor Law to Welfare State,* 84.

25 Trattner, *From Poor Law to Welfare State,* 90, n. 14.

26 Katz, *Shadow of the Poorhouse,* 56.

27 There is a small component of AFDC for intact families in which the principal earner is unemployed. AFDC is 90% female-headed.

28 Wisconsin State Board of Charities and Reform, *Third Biennial Report, 1887–1888* (1889), 184.

29 Alice Kessler-Harris, *Out to Work: A History of Wage-Earning Women in the United States* (New York: Oxford University Press, 1982).

30 See Nancy Fraser and Linda Gordon, "A Genealogy of Dependency: Tracing a Keyword of the U.S. Welfare State," *Signs* 19 (1994): 309–37.

31 Linda Gordon, *Pitied But Not Entitled* (New York: Free Press, 1994).

32 Gordon, *Pitied But Not Entitled;* Kessler-Harris, *Out to Work,* 1982.

33 Gordon, *Pitied But Not Entitled,* 84–87.

34 Linda Gordon, *Heroes of Their Own Lives: The Politics and History of Family Violence—Boston, 1880–1960* (New York: Viking, 1988), 82–108; see also Katz, *Shadow of the Poorhouse,* chap. 5.

35 Gordon, *Heroes of Their Own Lives,* 82–115.

36 Winnifred Bell, *Aid to Dependent Children* (New York: Columbia University Press, 1965), 6–7; Mark Leff, "Consensus for Reform: The Mothers'-Pension Movement in the Progressive Era," *Social Service Review* 47 (1983): 397–417.

37 Only about 15% of state statutes used the term "mothers' pensions." The remainder read either "aid to dependent children" or "aid to mothers of dependent children." The statutes are listed in U.S. Department of Labor, *Children's Bureau,* Chart No. 3: A Tabular Summary of State Laws Relating to Public Aid to Children in Their Own Homes in Effect January 1, 1934 (Washington, D.C.: Children's Bureau, 1934).

38 Gordon, *Pitied But Not Entitled.*

39 "Proceedings of the Conference on the Care of Dependent Children," Washington, D.C., January 25–26, 1909, 60th Cong., 2d sess., *Senate Document No. 721* (Washington, D.C.: U.S. Government Printing Office, 1909), 8; Bell, *Aid to Dependent Children,* 4.

40 See, e.g., Irwin Garfinkel and Sara McLanahan, *Single Mothers and Their Children: A New American Dilemma* (Washington, D.C.: Urban Institute Press, 1986), 99.

41 Bell, *Aid to Dependent Children,* 6–8; Leff, "Consensus for Reform"; Joel Handler and Yeheskel Hasenfeld, *The Moral Construction of Poverty: American Welfare Reform* (Newbury Park, Calif.: Sage, 1991), 63–74; Margaret Rosenheim, "Vagrancy Concepts in Welfare Law," in *Law of the Poor,* ed. Jacobus Ten Broek (Berkeley: School of Law, University of California, 1966), 187–242.

42 Handler and Hasenfeld, *Moral Construction of Poverty,* 68–70; Gordon, *Pitied But Not Entitled,* 129.

43 U.S. Committee on Economic Security, *Social Security in America: The Factual Background of the Social Security Act as Summarized from Staff Reports to the Committee on Economic Security by the Social Security Board,* Social Security Board Publication No. 20 (Washington, D.C.: U.S. Government Printing Office, 1937), 161.

44 Handler and Hasenfeld, *Moral Construction of Poverty,* 76–79.

45 Bell, *Aid to Dependent Children,* 14; Handler and Hasenfeld, *Moral Construction of Poverty,* 71; Rosenheim, "Vagrancy Concepts in Welfare Law," 187.

46 Frances Piven and Richard Cloward, *Poor People's Movements: Why They Succeed, How They Fail* (New York: Pantheon, 1977), chap. 5.

47 David Ellwood, *Poor Support* (New York: Basic Books, 1988); Garfinkel and McLanahan, *Single Mothers and Their Children.*

48 The chief sponsor and legislator most identified with the Family Support Act of 1988 is Senator Patrick Moynihan.
49 John Myles, "Postwar Capitalism and the Extension of Social Security into a Retirement Wage," in *The Politics of Social Policy in the United States,* ed. Margaret Weir, Ann S. Orloff, and Theda Skocpol (Princeton, N.J.: Princeton University Press, 1988), 265–92.
50 Theda Skocpol and Jill Ikenberry, "The Political Formation of the American Welfare State," *Comparative Social Research* 6 (1983): 87–148; Sheldon Danziger and Peter Gottschalk, "Unemployment Insurance and the Safety Net for the Unemployed," in *Unemployment Insurance: The Second Half-Century,* ed. W. Lee Hansen and James F. Byers (Madison: University of Wisconsin Press, 1990), 118–42.
51 Deborah Stone, *The Disabled State* (Philadelphia: Temple University Press, 1984).

Chapter 3: The Problem of Poverty, the Problem of Work

1 For a recent synthesis and analysis of the literature dealing with at-risk youth, see National Research Council (NRC), *Losing Generations: Adolescents at Risk* (Washington, D.C.: National Academy Press, 1993).
2 Denton Vaughan, "Exploring the Use of the Public's Views to Set Income Poverty Thresholds and Adjust Them over Time," *Social Security Bulletin* 56 (1993): 22–46.
3 U.S. House of Representatives, Committee on Ways and Means, *1993 Green Book: Background Material and Data on Programs within the Jurisdiction of the Committee on Ways and Means* (Washington, D.C.: U.S. Government Printing Office, 1993), 1307 (hereinafter cited as *1993 Green Book*).
4 Hugh Heclo, "Poverty Politics," in *Confronting Poverty: Prescriptions for Change,* ed. Sheldon Danziger, Gary Sandefur, and Daniel Weinberg (Cambridge, Mass.: Harvard University Press, 1994), 420.
5 *1993 Green Book,* 615, 1308. Poverty rates for children declined substantially from about 1960 until the mid-1970s and then began to increase steadily in the 1980s. Tom Corbett, "Learnfare: The Wisconsin Experience," *Focus* 12 (1989): 2.
6 Richard Freeman, "Employment and Earnings of Disadvantaged Youth in a Labor Shortage Economy," in *The Urban Underclass,* ed. Christopher Jencks and Paul E. Peterson (Washington, D.C.: Brookings Institution, 1991), 103–21.
7 NRC, *Losing Generations,* chap. 2.
8 *1993 Green Book,* 1308.
9 NRC, *Losing Generations,* 45 and see chaps. 2, 3; U.S. National Commission on Children, *Beyond Rhetoric: A New Agenda for Children and Families* (Washington, D.C.: U.S. National Commission on Children, 1991), chap. 2.
10 David Ellwood, *Poor Support* (New York: Basic Books, 1988), chap. 4.
11 Sara McLanahan and Gary Sandefur, *Growing Up with a Single Parent* (Cambridge, Mass.: Harvard University Press, 1994), 154.
12 McLanahan and Sandefur, *Growing Up,* 33–34.
13 NRC, *Losing Generations,* chap. 6.
14 Uri Bronfenbrenner, "What Do Families Do?" *Family Affairs* 1/2 (1991): 4.
15 Sanford M. Dornbusch, J. Merrill Carlsmith, Steven J. Bushwall, Phillip L. Ritter,

Herbert Leiderman, Albert H. Hastorf, and Ruth T. Gross, "Single Parents, Extended Households, and the Control of Adolescents," *Child Development* 56 (1985): 326–41.
16 National Commission on Children, *Beyond Rhetoric.*
17 Mark Testa, "Racial and Ethnic Variation in the Early Life Course of Adolescent Welfare Mothers," in *Early Parenthood and Coming of Age in the 1990s,* ed. Margaret K. Rosenheim and Mark F. Testa (New Brunswick, N.J.: Rutgers University Press, 1992), 89–112.
18 NRC, *Losing Generations,* 56.
19 See, e.g., U.S. Bureau of National Affairs, *Daily Labor Report* (Washington, D.C.: Bureau of National Affairs, 1994), chap. 3 (hereinafter cited as *Daily Labor Report*); McKinley Blackburn, David Bloom, and Richard Freeman, "The Declining Economic Position of Less Skilled American Men," in *A Future of Lousy Jobs? The Changing Structure of U.S. Wages,* ed. Gary Burtless (Washington, D.C.: Brookings Institution, 1990); Rebecca Blank, "The Employment Strategy: Public Policies to Increase Work and Earnings," in *Confronting Poverty: Prescriptions for Change,* ed. Sheldon Danziger, Gary Sandefur, and Daniel Weinberg (Cambridge, Mass.: Harvard University Press, 1994), 168–204; and Lawrence Mishel and David Frankel, *The State of Working America, 1990–91* (Armonk, N.Y.: M. E. Sharpe, 1991). It has been noted that even as productivity has risen, wages have remained stagnant or declined. Steven Pearlstein, "Recovery's Weak Spot Is Wages," *Washington Post,* March 9, 1994, 1.
20 Robert Haveman and John Sholz, "Transfers, Taxes, and Welfare Reform," *National Tax Journal* 47 (1994): 419, table 1.
21 Blank, "Employment Strategy," 173.
22 Jason DeParle, "Sharp Increase along the Borders of Poverty," *New York Times,* March 31, 1994, A8.
23 *Daily Labor Report.*
24 NRC, *Losing Generations,* chap. 2; see also *Daily Labor Report,* 25–26.
25 Blank, "Employment Strategy," table 3.
26 NRC, *Losing Generations,* chap. 2.
27 *Daily Labor Report,* 25.
28 NRC, *Losing Generations,* chap. 2.
29 NRC, *Losing Generations,* chap. 2; *Daily Labor Report,* 14.
30 According to Richard Freeman, at any one time, 18% of all 18–24-year-old dropouts and 30% of 25–34-year-old dropouts are under the supervision of the criminal justice system. For African Americans, the figures are 42% of 18–24-year-old dropouts and more than 75% of 24–34-year-old dropouts. Freeman, "Employment and Earnings of Disadvantaged Youth."
31 U.S. House of Representatives, Committee on Ways and Means, *1992 Green Book: Background Material and Data on Programs within the Jurisdiction of the Committee on Ways and Means* (Washington, D.C.: U.S. Government Printing Office, 1992; hereinafter cited as *1992 Green Book*), 555–56.
32 NRC, *Losing Generations,* chap. 2.

33 U.S. Government Accounting Office, *Workers at Risk* (Washington, D.C.: Government Accounting Office, 1991; herein after cited as *Workers at Risk*); *Daily Labor Report,* 28–29.
34 Rebecca Blank, "Are Part-Time Jobs Bad Jobs?" in *A Future of Lousy Jobs? The Changing Structure of U.S. Wages,* ed. Gary Burtless (Washington, D.C.: Brookings Institution, 1990).
35 David Lewin, "Institute of Industrial Relations, UCLA," *Time,* February 1, 1993, 53.
36 Involuntary part-time workers are those who report that they want full-time employment and are working part-time because they can find only part-time work or "slack work" or other reasons. Voluntary part-time workers are primarily those who say they do not want or are unavailable for full-time work. *Workers at Risk,* 17, n. 1.
37 Karen Holden, "Comment," in *A Future of Lousy Jobs? The Changing Structure of U.S. Wages,* ed. Gary Burtless (Washington, D.C.: Brookings Institution, 1990), 156.
38 Holden, "Comment."
39 Chris Tilly, *Short Hours, Short Shrift: Causes and Consequences of Part-Time Work* (Washington, D.C.: Economic Policy Institute, 1990), 5–6; David Lewin and Daniel Mitchell, *Alternative Approaches to Workplace Flexibility in the U.S.A.* (UCLA Institute of Industrial Relations, Reprint Series, 1992), 432.
40 Tilly, *Short Hours, Short Shrift,* 9; *Daily Labor Report,* 28.
41 *Workers at Risk,* 5–6.
42 Heclo, "Poverty Politics," 428–29.
43 U.S. House of Representatives, Committee on Ways and Means, *1994 Green Book: Background Material and Data on Programs within the Jurisdiction of the Committee on Ways and Means* (Washington, D.C.: U.S. Government Printing Office, 1994; hereinafter cited as *1994 Green Book*), 324–25.
44 *1994 Green Book,* 5, 125, 796.
45 *1994 Green Book,* 395.
46 These are 1992 figures; *1994 Green Book,* 399.
47 *1994 Green Book,* 399.
48 *1994 Green Book,* 324.
49 *1994 Green Book,* 399.
50 *1994 Green Book,* 401.
51 *1994 Green Book,* 401.
52 Maris Vinoskis, "Historical Perspectives on Adolescent Pregnancy," in *Early Parenthood and Coming of Age in the 1990s,* ed. Margaret Rosenheim and Mark Testa (New Brunswick, N.J.: Rutgers University Press, 1992).
53 *1994 Green Book,* 402.
54 *1994 Green Book,* 402.
55 Gary Burtless, "Paychecks or Welfare Checks: Can AFDC Recipients Support Themselves?" *Brookings Review,* Fall 1994, 35–37.
56 *1994 Green Book,* 440.
57 Peter Gottschalk, Sara McLanahan, and Gary Sandefur, "The Dynamics and Intergenerational Transmission of Poverty," in *Confronting Poverty: Prescriptions for Change,*

ed. Sheldon Danziger, Gary Sandefur, and Daniel Weinberg (Cambridge, Mass.: Harvard University Press, 1994), 85–108.

58 Mark Greenberg, *Beyond Stereotypes: What State AFDC Studies on Length of Stay Tell Us about Welfare as a "Way of Life"* (Washington, D.C.: Center for Law and Social Policy, 1993), i; LaDonna Pavetti, "The Dynamics of Welfare and Work: Exploring the Process by Which Women Work Their Way Off Welfare" (Ph.D. diss., JFK School of Government, Harvard University, 1993). Monthly data studies are limited—about five states, plus several work demonstration projects—but although there is variation, the studies are consistent in overall patterns. They are also consistent with the U.S. Bureau of the Census's Survey of Income and Program Participation (SIPP), which reported that 53.5% of AFDC entrants exited within one year and 71.5% exited within two years. The median welfare spell was seven months for "AFDC or other cash assistance," e.g., General Assistance. Quoted in Greenberg, *Beyond Stereotypes,* 17.

59 Greenberg, *Beyond Stereotypes;* Pavetti, "Dynamics of Welfare and Work."

60 *1992 Green Book,* 686.

61 Mary Jo Bane and David Ellwood, *Welfare Realities: From Rhetoric to Reform* (Cambridge, Mass.: Harvard University Press, 1994), 51.

62 Kathleen Harris, "Work and Welfare among Single Mothers in Poverty," *American Journal of Sociology* 99 (1993): 317–52; Greenberg, *Beyond Stereotypes,* 1993; Pavetti, "Dynamics of Welfare and Work," 39.

63 Changes in marital status or the youngest child reaching eighteen each account for just over 10% of all exits. Greenberg, *Beyond Stereotypes,* 2.

64 Frank Furstenberg, "The Next Generation: The Children of Teenage Mothers Grow Up," in *Early Parenthood and Coming of Age in the 1990s,* ed. Margaret Rosenheim and Mark Testa (New Brunswick, N.J.: Rutgers University Press, 1992).

65 Furstenberg, "Next Generation."

66 Gottschalk, McLanahan, and Sandefur, "Dynamics and Intergenerational Transmission of Poverty," 107.

67 Christopher Jencks, *Rethinking Social Policy: Race, Poverty, and the Underclass* (Cambridge, Mass.: Harvard University Press, 1992), 204.

68 The sampling technique is described in Jencks, *Rethinking Social Poverty,* 206. Edin basically relied on introductions and recommendations to minimize refusals and evasions. She also had to oversample to get enough whites. The final sample was 46% African American, 38% European American, 10% Latin American, and 6% Asian American, which are similar to national figures. She also oversampled from subsidized housing so that rents actually paid would more closely resemble rents paid nationwide.

69 Christopher Jencks, *The Homeless* (Cambridge, Mass.: Harvard University Press, 1994), 111.

70 For example, in 1984–85, rents for low-budget families averaged $240 per month in the San Francisco Bay area and Los Angeles, $220 in New York and Philadelphia, and $175 in Chicago and Detroit. Jencks, *Rethinking Social Policy,* 212.

71 Jencks, *Homeless,* 1994.

72 Harris, "Work and Welfare."

73 Harris, "Work and Welfare," 333. See also Bane and Ellwood, *Welfare Realities,* 55–59.
74 Burtless, "Paychecks or Welfare Checks," 35.
75 Harris, "Work and Welfare," 349; see also Bane and Ellwood, *Welfare Realities;* Greenberg, *Beyond Stereotypes;* and Pavetti, "Dynamics of Welfare and Work."

Chapter 4: Setting the Poor to Work

1 See Joel Handler and Yeheskel Hasenfeld, *The Moral Construction of Poverty: American Welfare Reform* (Newbury Park, Calif.: Sage, 1991), 120.
2 Handler and Hasenfeld, *Moral Construction of Poverty,* 141.
3 Handler and Hasenfeld, *Moral Construction of Poverty,* p. 146–54.
4 Handler and Hasenfeld, *Moral Construction of Poverty,* 154–58.
5 Handler and Hasenfeld, *Moral Construction of Poverty,* 170–73.
6 Handler and Hasenfeld, *Moral Construction of Poverty,* 179–86.
7 U.S. General Accounting Office, *Work and Welfare* (Washington, D.C.: U.S. General Accounting Office, 1986).
8 Daniel Friedlander, Gregory Hoerz, Janet Quint, and James Riccio, *Arkansas: Final Report on the WORK Program in Two Counties* (New York: Manpower Demonstration Research Corporation, 1985).
9 Barbara Goldman, Daniel Friedlander, Judith Gueron, and David Long, *California—The Demonstration of State Work/Welfare Initiatives: Findings from the San Diego Job Search and Work Experience Demonstration* (New York: Manpower Demonstration Research Corporation, 1985).
10 Gayle Hamilton and Daniel Friedlander, *Saturated Work Initiative Model in San Diego* (New York: Manpower Demonstration Research Corporation, 1989).
11 June O'Neill, *Work and Welfare in Massachusetts: An Evaluation of the ET Program* (Boston, Mass.: Pioneer Institute for Public Policy Research, 1990); Stephen Savner, Lucy Williams, and Monica Halas, "The Massachusetts Employment Training Program," *Clearinghouse Review* 20 (1986): 123–31; Handler and Hasenfeld, *Moral Construction of Poverty,* 186–90.
12 Compare O'Neill, *Work and Welfare in Massachusetts,* with Demetra Smith Nightingale, Douglas A. Wissoker, Lynn C. Burbridge, D. Lee Bawden, and Neal Jeffries, *Evaluation of Massachusetts Employment Training (ET) Program* (Washington, D.C.: Urban Institute Press, 1991).
13 James Riccio, Barbara Goldman, Gayle Hamilton, Karin Martinson, and Alan Orenstein, *GAIN: Early Implementation Experiences and Lessons* (New York: Manpower Demonstration Research Corporation, 1989).
14 John Wallace and David Long, *GAIN: Planning and Early Implementation* (New York: Manpower Demonstration Research Corporation, 1987).
15 Handler and Hasenfeld, *Moral Construction of Poverty,* 196.
16 James Riccio, Daniel Friedlander, and Stephen Freedman, *Executive Summary, GAIN: Benefits, Costs, and Three-Year Impacts of a Welfare-to-Work Program* (New York: Manpower Demonstration Research Corporation, 1994).
17 There is a serious problem of equity here. One observer saw a middle-aged man ap-

proach the Riverside welfare department seeking employment. He was told that he had to be a welfare recipient. This illustrates the more general problem of providing services and benefits to people in special categories, such as welfare, and not to others in reasonably similar circumstances. Mark Greenberg (1994) calls this the "downward drag of equity." It comes up in the Learnfare programs that include incentives; see chapter 5.
18 County of Riverside Department of Public Social Services, *GAIN Program, Transferability Package for High Output Job Placement Results March* (Riverside, Calif.: Department of Public Social Services, 1994), 55–118.
19 Riccio et al., *Executive Summary GAIN,* ES-1–2.
20 In Year 3, individuals in the experimental group earned $1,010 more than the controls; in Year 1, the difference was $920, and in Year 2, $1,183. County of Riverside Department of Public Social Services, *GAIN Program,* table 1.
21 The net cost is the government's net expenditures after adding the costs of education and training that the individuals in the experimental group undertook on their own after leaving GAIN and subtracting the education and training costs that control subjects received on their own. Riccio et al., *Executive Summary, GAIN,* ES-3.
22 Daniel Friedlander, *The Impacts of California's GAIN Program on Different Ethnic Groups: Two-Year Findings on Earnings and AFDC Payments* (New York: Manpower Demonstration Research Corporation, 1994), iv.
23 John Kemple and Joshua Haimson, *Florida's Project Independence* (New York: Manpower Demonstration Research Corporation, 1994).
24 Mark Greenberg, *Welfare Reform on a Budget: What's Happening in JOBS* (Washington, D.C.: Center for Law and Social Policy, 1992).
25 U.S. House of Representatives, Committee on Ways and Means, *1994 Green Book: Background Material and Data on Programs within the Jurisdiction of the Committee on Ways and Means* (Washington, D.C.: U.S. Government Printing Office, 352; hereinafter cited as *1994 Green Book*).
26 Greenberg 1992; *1994 Green Book,* 352.
27 Karen Martinson and Daniel Friedlander, *GAIN: Basic Education in a Welfare-to-Work Program* (New York: Manpower Demonstration Research Corporation, 1994), xviii. The report is based on a sample of more than 2,500 welfare recipients.
28 Kathleen Harris, "Work and Welfare among Single Mothers in Poverty," *American Journal of Sociology* 99 (1993): 317–52; LaDonna Pavetti, "The Dynamics of Welfare and Work: Exploring the Process by Which Women Work Their Way Off Welfare" (Ph.D. diss., JFK School of Government, Harvard University, 1993).
29 Martin and Friedlander, *GAIN,* xvii.
30 TALS uses written materials encountered in everyday life—schedules, maps, want ads—to assess an individual's understanding and problem-solving ability. MDRC used TALS on the basis of expert opinion that it is an appropriate test for disadvantaged adults, has a high statistical reliability, and has been used nationally, thus affording an ability to compare GAIN recipients with other groups. Martinson and Friedlander, *GAIN,* xxiii.
31 Pavetti, "Dynamics of Welfare and Work."

32 Handler and Hasenfeld, *Moral Construction of Poverty,* 200, n. 2.

33 Gordon Lafer, "The Politics of Job Training: Urban Poverty and the False Promise of JTPA," *Politics and Society* 22 (1994): 349–388, n. 76.

34 Lafer, "Politics of Job Training," 356.

35 Reporting substantial job loss are Mark Greenberg, *Beyond Stereotypes: What State AFDC Studies on Length of Stay Tell Us about Welfare as a "Way of Life"* (Washington, D.C.: Center for Law and Social Policy, 1993); Harris, "Work and Welfare"; and Pavetti, "Dynamics of Welfare and Work."

36 Greenberg, *Beyond Stereotypes.*

37 Greenberg, *Beyond Stereotypes.*

38 *1994 Green Book,* 358–59.

39 Judith Gueron, "Welfare and Poverty: Strategies to Increase Work," paper presented at conference, "Reducing Poverty in America," Anderson Graduate School of Management, UCLA, January 15–16, 1993.

40 Gueron, "Welfare and Poverty."

41 Christopher Jencks, *Rethinking Social Policy: Race, Poverty, and the Underclass* (Cambridge, Mass.: Harvard University Press, 1992), 222.

42 Jencks, *Rethinking Social Policy,* 226. Jencks has not counted the Earned Income Tax Credit, which may make a substantial difference. I discuss the EITC in chapter 7.

43 Pavetti, "Dynamics of Welfare and Work."

44 California Department of Public Social Services, *Final Report to GAIN Advisory Council Members,* September 8, 1994.

45 California Department of Public Social Services, *Final Report.*

46 L. Udesky, "Punishing the Poor," *Southern Exposure,* Summer 1991, 12–13; Leonard Goodwin, *Causes and Cures of Welfare* (Lexington, Mass.: Lexington Books, 1983).

47 Harris, "Work and Welfare," 345.

48 Lawrence Mead, *Beyond Entitlement: The Social Obligations of Citizenship* (New York: Free Press, 1986).

49 Kathleen Harris, "Teenage Mothers and Welfare Dependency," *Journal of Family Issues* 12 (1991): 502–4.

50 Yeheskel Hasenfeld and Dale Weaver, *Enforcement, Compliance and Disputes in Welfare-to-Work Programs* (Los Angeles: UCLA School of Social Welfare, Center for Child and Family Studies, 1993).

Chapter 5: The Return to the States

Note to epigraph: Congressional Record, 100th Cong., 2d sess., 136, pt. 14:416–17, October 3, 1990 (daily ed.).

1 See Mark Greenberg, *Contract with Disaster: The Impact on States of the Personal Responsibility Act* (Washington, D.C.: Center for Law and Social Policy, 1994); Lucy Williams, "The Ideology of Division: Behavior Modification Welfare Reform Proposals," *Yale Law Journal* 102 (1992): 719–46; Lucy Williams, "The Abuse of Section 1115 Waivers: Welfare Reform without a Standard," *Yale Law and Policy Review* 12 (1994): 8–37; Michael Wiseman, "Welfare Reform in the States: The Bush Legacy," *Focus* 15

(1993): 18–36; Jason DeParle, "States' Eagerness to Experiment on Welfare Jars Administration," *New York Times,* March 14, 1994, A1.

2 Center for Social Welfare Policy and Law, "Welfare Reform?" *Center for Social Welfare Policy and Law News,* October 1994, 5.

3 U.S. House of Representatives, Committee on Ways and Means, *1994 Green Book: Background Material and Data on Programs within the Jurisdiction of the Committee on Ways and Means* (Washington, D.C.: U.S. Government Printing Office, 1994; hereinafter cited as *1994 Green Book*), 324–25.

4 Linda Gordon, *Pitied But Not Entitled* (New York: Free Press, 1994).

5 Williams, "Abuse of Section 1115 Waivers," 12–13.

6 For a time, there was some effort to apply human subjects protections to welfare waivers, but HHS, under President Reagan, rejected that position. Williams, "Abuse of Section 1115 Waivers," 21–24.

7 Williams, "Abuse of Section 1115 Waivers," 17; Stuart Butler, "How the White House Spurs Welfare Reform," *Heritage Foundation Backgrounder* 705 (1989): 10.

8 Williams, "Abuse of Section 1115 Waivers," 18, n. 54.

9 Jason DeParle, "Clinton Allows State to Limit Aid to Indigent," *New York Times,* November 2, 1993, 1.

10 Interview with Mark Greenberg, Center for Law and Social Policy, Washington, D.C., November 1994.

11 DeParle, "States' Eagerness," A1.

12 See Wiseman, "Welfare Reform in the States," 33.

13 DeParle, "States' Eagerness," A12.

14 Williams, "Abuse of Section 1115 Waivers," 26–27.

15 Jason DeParle, "Wisconsin Pledges to Exit U.S. System of Public Welfare," *New York Times,* December 14, 1993, A1. It should be noted that AFDC in Wisconsin has been declining 10% a year since 1988.

16 Wiseman, "Welfare Reform in the States," 32.

17 *Beno v Shalala,* 9th Cir. 1994.

18 It was a 2–1 decision. HHS has great discretion in granting these waivers. The majority, although it was extremely skeptical of experimental claims for the waiver, found that the record did not indicate that HHS exercised any discretion, that is, the government failed to consider at all the plaintiffs' claims that the waivers, among other things, would cause harm to large classes of AFDC recipients. In the only other case to consider the waiver policy, the court of appeals for the Second Circuit upheld HHS on the grounds that a state memorandum answering the plaintiffs' objections to the proposed waiver was in the record. This satisfied the appellate court that the secretary of HHS had exercised discretion. *Aguayo v Richardson,* 473 F2d 1090 (2d Cir) 1973. This is very limited judicial review. There is litigation in other states, however. DeParle, "Wisconsin Pledges to Exit," A12.

19 The appellate court doubted that the claimed work-incentives effects of the cuts would not have an impact on the disabled and on certain categories of children. Accordingly, the state modified its waiver request to exclude these two groups, estimated to be about

8.4% of the state AFDC population. The rest would be cut. Virginia Ellis, "Wilson Offers Concessions to Preserve Cuts in Welfare," *Los Angeles Times*, August 27, 1994, A24.
20 Williams, "Ideology of Division," 727.
21 Williams, "Ideology of Division," 733.
22 Quoted in Williams, "Ideology of Division," 729.
23 Williams, "Ideology of Division," 731.
24 David Long, Robert Wood, and Hilary Kopp with Rebecca Fisher, *LEAP: The Educational Effects of LEAP and Enhanced Services in Cleveland* (New York: Manpower Demonstration Research Corporation, 1994).
25 Teens can be excused if they are in the last seven months of pregnancy, caring for a child under three months, or unable to obtain either transportation or child care.
26 Long et al., *LEAP*, 26.
27 Long et al., *LEAP*, 28.
28 Long et al., *LEAP*, 34.
29 Long et al., *LEAP*, 52.
30 Long et al., *LEAP*, 84.
31 Long et al., *LEAP*, vi.
32 U.S. Department of Commerce, *Current Population Reports, Population Characteristics: Marital Status and Living Arrangements, March 1993* (Washington, D.C.: U.S. Government Printing Office, 1994).
33 Sara McLanahan and Gary Sandefur, *Growing Up with a Single Parent* (Cambridge, Mass.: Harvard University Press, 1994).
34 Williams, "Ideology of Division," 740.
35 DeParle, "Wisconsin Pledges to Exit."
36 Exceptions include disability, caring for a disabled person, being in the last trimester of pregnancy, caring for a child under age two, being a recipient under age twenty in high school full-time, and being a nonrecipient caretaker of welfare children.

Chapter 6: The Current Reform Proposals

1 Jason DeParle, "The Clinton Welfare Bill Begins Trek in Congress," *New York Times*, July 15, 1994, A10.
2 Marshall Will and Martin Schram, eds., *Mandate for Change* (New York: Berkley Books, 1993).
3 William Clinton and Albert Gore, *Putting People First* (New York: Times Books, 1993).
4 David Ellwood, *Poor Support* (New York: Basic Books, 1988).
5 For example, during her confirmation hearings to become secretary of HHS, Donna Shalala was sharply criticized by liberal Democrats for not discussing welfare reform. The *New York Times* cover story and subsequent editorial about the Shalala hearings described Clinton's welfare reform only in terms of "ending welfare as we know it." *New York Times*, January 15, 1993, A15.
6 Mark Greenberg, *The Devil Is in the Details* (Washington, D.C.: Center for Law and Social Policy, 1992).
7 Greenberg, *Devil Is in the Details.*
8 The twenty-four-month clock can be extended under certain circumstances. Examples

include cases where education and training cannot be completed because of the state's failure to provide or arrange for child care or other services previously agreed to, individuals receiving special education until they achieve the equivalent of a high school education or reach age twenty-two, and individuals enrolled in special learning programs designed to lead to a degree or recognized skills certificate. States may opt to grant extensions for up to twelve months to complete high school and twenty-four months for a postsecondary program if the individual is enrolled in a work-study program and making "satisfactory progress," which is not defined. Again, there are penalties and exceptions if the states exceed 10% of the extensions to the phase-in group.

The twenty-four-month time on welfare will be cumulative over the life of the recipient. There are various rules to count the time that is used up. In most cases, if a recipient were to leave welfare after having been on welfare for eighteen or more months, she would not be able to get AFDC without participating in the work requirement. There are rules for "earning back" some time. Greenberg writes, "If an individual left AFDC with more than 18 months counting against the 24 month clock, then the number would be reduced by one month for every four months in which the individual did not receive AFDC or participate in the WORK program. However, the months on the clock for such a person would never fall below 18." Mark Greenberg, *Contract with Disaster: The Impact on States of the Personal Responsibility Act* (Washington, D.C.: Center for Law and Social Policy, 1994).

9 Greenberg, *Devil Is in the Details,* 7.

10 Jason DeParle, "Change in Welfare Is Likely to Need Big Jobs Program," *New York Times,* November 30, 1994, 1.

11 DeParle, "Change in Welfare."

12 Tracy Kaplan, "Jobs Scarce for Recipients of 'Workfare,'" *Los Angeles Times,* June 24, 1994, B1.

13 Gary Burtless, "Are Targeted Wage Subsidies Harmful? Evidence From a Wage Voucher Experiment," *Industrial and Labor Relations Review* 39 (1985): 105–14.

14 Thomas Brock, David Butler, and David Long, *Unpaid Work Experience for Welfare Recipients: Findings and Lessons from MDRC Research* (Washington, D.C.: Manpower Demonstration Research Corporation, 1993).

15 Greenberg, *Devil Is in the Details.*

16 Greenberg, *Devil Is in the Details.*

17 Greenberg, *Devil Is in the Details,* 8.

18 Mark Greenberg, *Striking Out* (Washington, D.C.: Center for Law and Social Policy, 1994), 4–5, 16. AFDC-UP (Unemployed Parent) recipients would be required to participate in a JOBS component thirty-two hours per week and participate in job search eight hours.

19 Greenberg, *Contract with Disaster.*

20 Greenberg, *Contract with Disaster,* 15.

21 Ellen Galinsky, Carollee Howes, Susan Kantos, and Marybeth Shinn, *The Study of Children in Family Child Care and Relative Care: Highlights of Findings* (New York: Families and Work Institute, 1994), 205.

22 *Cost, Quality, and Child Outcomes in Child Care Centers: Executive Summary* (Univer-

sity of Colorado, University of California—Los Angeles, University of North Carolina, and Yale University, 1995).

23 Center for Social Policy and Law, "Welfare Reform?" *Center for Social Welfare Policy and Law News,* October 1994, 13.

24 Ellwood, *Poor Support.*

25 Gordon Lafer, "The Politics of Job Training: Urban Poverty and the False Promise of JTPA," *Politics and Society* 22 (1994): 349–88, quotation on 351.

26 Philip Harvey, "Welfare Reform, Human Rights, and the Future of Capitalism," Joanne Woodward Lecture, Sarah Lawrence College, April 6, 1994.

27 Gary Burtless, "Paychecks or Welfare Checks: Can AFDC Recipients Support Themselves?" *Brookings Review,* Fall 1994, 37.

28 Greenberg, *Contract with Disaster,* 30.

29 Fredrica Kramer, *From Quality Control to Quality Improvement in AFDC and Medicaid* (Washington, D.C.: National Academy Press, 1988), 82–93.

30 Joel Handler and Yeheskel Hasenfeld, *The Moral Construction of Poverty: American Welfare Reform* (Newbury Park, Calif.: Sage, 1991), 120.

31 See, for example, my description of the efforts of an advocate spending in excess of one hundred hours in trying to get a mentally ill recipient onto General Relief. Joel Handler, "The Transformation of Aid to Families with Dependent Children: The Family Support Act in Historical Context," *New York University Review of Law and Social Change* 16 (1987–88): 457, 529–33.

32 See Handler, "Transformation of Aid," 481, n. 109.

33 Kramer, *From Quality Control to Quality Improvement,* 2. The quality control system applied to Food Stamps and Medicaid as well as AFDC.

34 Interview with Deborah Chassman, then a senior official in HHS, March 1986.

35 Michael Lipsky, "Bureaucratic Disentitlement in Social Welfare Programs," *Social Service Review* 58 (1984): 2–27.

36 Mark Greenberg gives this example. The Congressional Budget Office estimates that the cost of placing a recipient in a thirty-five-hour-a-week job would exceed $6,000, including child care. A comparable WORK slot for six months would be $3,000. The median AFDC benefit for a family of three is $367; adding the $120 work expense disregard equals $2,922 for the AFDC cost for six months. Greenberg, *Contract with Disaster,* 31.

37 Yeheskel Hasenfeld and Dale Weaver, "Enforcement, Compliance, and Disputes in Welfare-to-Work Programs," UCLA Center for Child and Family Studies, 1993.

38 Greenberg, *Contract with Disaster,* 28–29.

39 The exceptions would be refugees during their first six years in the United States and persons admitted for lawful permanent residence who were over age seventy-five and had resided in the United States for five years.

Chapter 7: Another Exercise in Symbolic Politics

1 David Ellwood, *Poor Support* (New York: Basic Books, 1988), 180.

2 John Scholz, "Tax Policy and the Working Poor: The Earned Income Tax Credit," *Focus* 15 (1993–94): 2.

3 Robert Haveman and John Scholz, "Transfers, Taxes, and Welfare Reform," *National Tax Journal* 47 (1994): 417.

4 Ann Alstott, "The Earned Income Tax Credit and the Limitations of Tax-Based Welfare Reform," *Harvard Law Review* 108 (1995): 533; Barbara Kirchheimer, "The EITC: Where Policy and Practicality Collide," *Tax Notes,* October 3, 1994, 15–18.

5 Alstott, "Earned Income Tax Credit."

6 Mary Jo Bane and David Ellwood, *Welfare Realities: From Rhetoric to Reform* (Cambridge, Mass.: Harvard University Press, 1994), 1.

7 Bane and Ellwood, *Welfare Realities,* 25–26, 132. The specific chapters in which these arguments are made were written, respectively, by Bane and Thomas Kane and by Bane. I assume that as a coauthor of the entire volume, Ellwood does not disagree with Bane's analysis.

8 John Kincaid, "From Cooperative to Coercive Federalism," *Annals, AAPSS* 509 (1990): 139–52.

9 See Christopher Jencks, *The Homeless* (Cambridge, Mass.: Harvard University Press, 1994).

10 June Axinn and Herman Levin, *Social Welfare: A History of the American Response to Need* (New York: Dodd, Mead, 1975), 36–37.

Index